Madeline Leslie

Lost But Found

The Jewish Home

Madeline Leslie

Lost But Found
The Jewish Home

ISBN/EAN: 9783337029029

Printed in Europe, USA, Canada, Australia, Japan

Cover: Foto ©Thomas Meinert / pixelio.de

More available books at **www.hansebooks.com**

OR,

THE JEWISH HOME.

AUNT HATTIE.

BOSTON:
HENRY A. YOUNG & CO.,
No. 24 Cornhill.
1868.

Entered, according to Act of Congress, in the year 1866, by
GRAVES AND YOUNG,
In the Clerk's Office of the District Court of the District of Massachusetts.

TO

EMILY BLAGDEN, & CORNELIA LOUISE,

DAUGHTERS OF

MY BELOVED WASHINGTON

FRIENDS, MR. & MRS. COYLE, I DEDICATE

THIS VOLUME, IN THE HOPE THAT

IT MAY INCREASE THE INTEREST OF YOUR-

SELVES AND YOUR PARENTS IN GOD'S

ANCIENT PEOPLE, AND CAUSE YOU

TO LABOR AND PRAY MORE

EARNESTLY THAT THEIR

HEARTS MAY BE TURNED TO THE MESSIAH

PROMISED THEIR FATHERS.

CONTENTS.

CHAPTER I.
	PAGE.
THE ARRIVAL,	7

CHAPTER II.
| THE BROKEN BONE, | 17 |

CHAPTER III.
| PREJUDICED HEARTS, | 31 |

CHAPTER IV.
| THE CHILD PREACHER, | 47 |

CHAPTER V.
| PLEADING THE PROMISE, | 59 |

CHAPTER VI.
| MYSTERY INCREASING, | 70 |

CHAPTER VII.
| FROM PALACE TO PRISON, | 80 |

CHAPTER VIII.
| FROM HOME TO HOME, | 93 |

CHAPTER IX.
| SAD, YET REJOICING, | 105 |

CHAPTER X.
| HOME FROM PRISON, | 119 |

CHAPTER XI.
Home not Home,.................................... 133

CHAPTER XII.
The Jewish Christian Boy,...................... 144

CHAPTER XIII.
The Synagogue and Rabbi,..................... 156

CHAPTER XIV.
From Synagogue to Church,.................... 171

CHAPTER XV.
A Nail in a Sure Place,.......................... 188

CHAPTER XVI.
First Works,.. 202

CHAPTER XVII.
A New Apostle,................................... 214

CHAPTER XVIII.
Fruits of Piety,................................... 230

CHAPTER XIX.
The Right Son at Last,......................... 243

CHAPTER XX.
Visit to the Rabbi,.............................. 255

CHAPTER XXI.
Feast of Tabernacles, ... 268

LOST BUT FOUND.

CHAPTER I.

THE ARRIVAL.

OUR story commences with a scene in the quiet parlor of a widowed lady, living in one of the most lovely and prosperous villages in the Western part of New York State. Her name is Duncan; and at the present moment she is giving a visitor an account of the last Sabbath School Concert, when a lad of twelve bounds into the room exclaiming:

"Mamma! they have come! I saw a load of furniture going into the gate, and ran like sixty after it, when I met a gentleman and two little girls coming down the avenue. Oh, but he's a cross man!"

"'What do you want boy,' he said, in an awful stern voice."

" Remember these are private grounds now."

" And what did you reply, Isaac?"

" I was so frightened, I couldn't say any thing. I looked at the little girls a minute, and wondered how they dared cling so to his hand; and then I ran home as fast as I could."

The lady rose, and advancing to the window, raised the shade so that she could overlook the grounds of her new neighbor, at the same time a flush of excitement tinged her usually pale cheek.

" I am mortified, my dear," she urged in a very gentle voice, " that you should have gone into the grounds."

" But, mamma, you've always given me leave to roll my hoop there," interrupted the boy.

"Yes; Isaac, but that was when the place was owned by my brother, and had no tenant.—We have no right there now."

The lad looked disappointed, and was only partially relieved when the visitor, Miss Roby remarked:

"I suppose you will make an early call on your new neighbors. Do you know any thing of them?"

"Only their name, which is a foreign one. Mr. Seixas made the purchase through his agent. I am glad he has children."

"They looked exactly alike, mamma."

"Probably they are twins. Are they pretty?"

"I think so. Their eyes are real black, and twinkle like stars; and their complexions are just like mine," the boy added, laughing; "and that is like a spaniard you say; but I think they're splendid."

Taking a seat at the window, Isaac interested himself the next half hour in watching the progress of unloading the furniture at the door of the house opposite. Though Mrs. Duncan's house, as well as her neighbor's, were each set back from the street, with avenues winding up to the front door, the lawns in front being dotted with ornamental trees and shrubs; yet a vista, directly in the line of the front entrances, allowed a clear view of one from the other. In the structure of the two buildings, and the general laying out of the grounds, the places were very similar, the one just sold having been built and for many years occupied by Mrs. Duncan's only brother. For two years, however, the house had been unoccupied, as Mr. Edwards was in Europe, from whence he might at any time return and take possession.

About two months previous to this, the lady had a letter from him stating that he had through his agent a good offer for the place, and as it was now probable that he might be obliged to remain abroad several years longer, he had concluded to sell. He knew nothing at all of the purchaser, except that he was a man of great wealth by the name of Seixas.

Under these circumstances it was not strange that Isaac felt at liberty to enter the grounds, every foot of which was as familiar to him as their own place; nor that Mrs. Duncan was greatly interested to learn the character of the new comers.

But for the present she seated herself by her friend, and with her crotcheting in hand went quietly on with her account of the meeting.

"The most interesting part of the exercises to me," she resumed, "was the class from the ragged school under the care of Miss Stewart. Our minister catechised them, and really it was surprising how much they had learned in the short time she has had them under her instruction."

"Oh, mamma! there is a splendid great harp going in," shouted Isaac, his whole face blazing with excitement. — "The little girls are carrying in the covers, I wish — Can't I go over and help them?"

Mrs. Duncan smiled at his enthusiasm, but said gently, "no my dear!"

The eagerness with which he asked the question, starting to his feet and catching his cap from the chair, and the manner in which he received the denial, told a volume regarding the mother's disipline.

Without a word of urging, without even a sullen look, the boy resumed his seat and his watching, and presently he found enough to occupy him, for before the first wagon had moved from the door two others, heavily loaded, came toiling up the avenue.

"They must be very rich, mamma, come here, please, and see what heaps and heaps of things."

It was almost dark before the last wagon rolled away, but still Isaac could see the little girls running here and there, singing and shouting to their father.

At last a woman came from the house and led them in. "What will they have for supper?" he inquired in dismay. "I suppose they wont have time to cook any thing."

Mrs. Duncan, ever mindful of the wants of others, had thought the same, and much relieved her son by saying: "I have already sent to offer assistance. John carried in a basket of bread, pies and cold meat but they were already supplied from the Wistar House."

She did not consider it necessary to add what had ruffled her own temper, that her servant was very coldly received, and returned with scarcely a civil answer from Mr Seixas, who happened to be passing through the entry and opened the door.

"Tell your mistress," he said, "that we do

not wish her food,—that it is easy to supply ourselves from the public house near by, and that we have all the help we need." Not one word showing his appreciation of her kindness, but a desire to assert at once and forever his independence of any one.

Mrs. Duncan was a Christian; not merely in name, but in her daily life. She acted out the principles she found revealed in the Scriptures. She was a diligent reader of the Bible; and she found this precept from the lips of her Lord: "Judge not that ye be not judged; for with what judgment ye judge ye shall be judged, and with what measure ye mete, it shall be measured to you again."

It was the thought of this precept which enabled her to curb her indignation when she found how her kindness had been received, and to say to the servant,—angry in her behalf:

"Never mind, John. We have done right, according to the golden rule; for I am sure in their circumstances, I should have been glad of such an offer. Mr. Seixas is probably a foreigner, and perhaps not being accustomed to these acts of neighborly kindness, he may consider them intrusive."

"I hope ye'll not be sending them civil speeches by me again, ma'am," urged the man. "I'd be afraid they'd turn to angry ones before I spoke them."

"Take care, John," was the pleasant rejoinder. "You know, I told you, 'tisn't angry words addressed to us which hurt us. It is only angry thoughts swelling up in our own hearts, and cherished there. If you feel disturbed by Mr. Seixas's incivility you must try and find all the excuses for him in your power."

"Tisn't human natur, ma'am; and I'm free to say, if some accident happens to his nice furniture that sets him up so, I'd not be the fellow to lament over it, and there's the truth for ye, ma'am."

"Oh, John, I'm grieved for you! Don't you remember how I explained the sixth commandment to you? It is not only actual murder which our Saviour forbids, but anger toward our neighbor."

"It's no use trying to make myself out to be what I'm not, Miss. Duncan," replied John, fidgetting and twirling the empty basket over his head. "I'd be glad, since it displeases you to be sweet on the new folks, but natur's natur."

"Yes, John; and grace is grace. You are not required to live by your own strength."

CHAPTER II.

THE BROKEN BONE.

IN a country village, every one feels at liberty to inquire into the affairs of his neighbors; and so whenever the servants of Mr Seixas made their appearance at the stores or the Post Office, many eager questions were put to them concerning the motives of their master in locating in their town, — the reason he came at this particular time, — the number of his family, — and the probability of his proving an acquisition to the place. But both nurse and butler had been in Mr. Seixas's employ for many years, and were far too shrewd to answer these questions in a satisfactory manner. Indeed, the nurse whom the twins called Abigail, was so rude and defiant in manner, that few felt inclined with her to venture upon a second interrogatory, while the man who condescendingly informed the grocer that he might be addressed as Mr. Powers, so carefully guarded his answers as to arouse still greater curiosity.

For the next month little was talked of but the strangers, while rumors, founded on the most trivial circumstances, were circulated from mouth to mouth until the worst character was ascribed to the whole family.

"I wish people wouldn't talk so," exclaimed Isaac Duncan rushing into his mother's parlor, out of breath with his haste, — I think the little Seixas girls are real nice; but Georgey Hand says he wouldn't speak to them for any thing. He says that his father has found out that Mr. Siexas is a wicked man who has been in prison."

"I suspect Mr. Hand knows no more about

the gentleman than we do," replied Mrs. Duncan with a smile. "I was walking out yesterday and their carriage passed me slowly. A lady was in it, very pale and thin, most tenderly supported and addressed by a gentleman, whom, though I did not see his face, I suppose, was Mr. Seixas. It is only natural to infer that she was mother to the twins who were on the opposite seat talking sweetly together. I saw that though she looked extremely ill, her glance rested lovingly on them. Probably it is on her account they moved to this place where they hoped to obtain quiet and good air."

Isaac listened eagerly, as he always did when their new neighbors were mentioned, and then exclaimed with a sigh:

"How I wish I'd been there. Was the nurse there, too?'

"No, dear, the carriage was a phæton, and

held only four, beside the high seat for the driver."

"I'm so glad he is kind to his wife," murmured the child thoughtfully, after gazing at the house for some minutes. "And the twins seemed happy. I wish I knew their names."

However much Mr. Seixas might desire to seclude himself, it was scarcely possible to live entirely independent of others; and in time it gradually leaked out — that, the family were very wealthy, and lived in grand style, — that Mrs. Seixas was a confirmed invalid, — that the twins answered to the names of Myrtilla and Esther, — that they had lived in Europe for several years, and that Mr. and Mrs. Seixas though rich were not happy.

During the summer, one of the servants was taken ill, and her place was temporarily supplied by a young girl from the village, who, though she asked no questions, kept herself wide awake to learn all she could of the mystery in which the family had shrouded themselves.

She did not stay long, for Abigail, who during the sickness of her mistress, exercised a general control over the whole household, was so cross and difficult to please, and so constantly finding fault with the new servant, that the girl declared no money would tempt her to bear such treatment.

During the summer, too, Mr. Seixas purchased a valuable piece of land adjoining his grounds, and began to lay it out in walks and groves in an expensive manner. As he was obliged to hire laborers, this brought him in contact with different individuals, and the result was, that his popularity as a gentleman and a neighbor was not increased. Indeed, one and another openly declared that he had obtained the land which belonged to children under age, by unlawful means, — that he had bribed their guardian into the bargain, — that he was social and friendly while he had an object to obtain, and then distant and cold; in short, that there was something concealed,— and this something must be guilt.

Mrs. Duncan heard many of these rumors, for she mingled freely in the society of the village; but principle triumphed over the natural disposition to judge her neighbors.

She had a warm, affectionate heart, and when she heard of Mr. Seixas's sternness, and severity to his servants, his want of liberality to the poor, his endeavor to obtain the services of those he employed at the lowest possible wages, her thoughts often recurred to the scene in the carriage. It was too real to deceive any one.

"Surely," she said to herself, as, sitting by her chamber window she watched the half drawn curtains in the room of the invalid, "a man who is so good a husband cannot be wholly corrupt."

Isaac had from the first, notwithstanding the summary dismissal he had received, been a warm champion in defence of the whole family. Even the surly Abigail received her share of praise. Mrs. Duncan often smiled to herself as she listened to the animated discussion between her son and the misused John, who had never forgiven the return made to his mistress' politeness. " Don't tell me," he insisted again and again. "Sure and it's little learning I got when I was a lad; but I'd hide my head in the ground any day when I couldn't know better than to treat a lady and the servant of a lady in that style. Feth, master Isaac, it's yerself that can convince me of many things; but ye can't bring me to the conviction that the man beyond is a gintleman at all." Strange enough, Isaac was the first one to form an acquaintance with the family.

It was early in the month of June that

he was returning from a distant part of the town where he had been on an errand for his mother, when he saw the twins in company with their nurse running across a field toward the road pursued by a ferocious bull that was pastured there.

Quick as thought the brave boy sprang over the wall shouting to the woman to take off her red scarf which attracted the creature toward her, and seizing a stone ran closely before the animal.

It was a hazardous experiment, and for one instant he realized the danger of encountering the infuriated beast; but he was a brave boy, and thought if he could succeed in keeping him at bay until they were out of reach, he could by some means escape injury to himself. Myrtilla and her sister, screaming and shrieking for help, ran toward the wall and were safe; but Abigail encumbered with a basket, into which she had now crowded the flaming garment, was less nimble. One glance in that direction, showed her on the top of the wall, and there she thought he might look out for his own safety. Making a sudden turn, he doubled and doubled, until he was near enough to the enclosure to run without fear of being overtaken, and soon fell over the wall completely exhausted.

His companions were now several rods distant,— and when he was a little recovered he approached them. One of the twins was stooping over nurse who sat on the ground groaning with pain, while her sister stood helplessly gazing at them, her countenance of a dreadful palor.

"Are you hurt?" asked Isaac, advancing eagerly.

Esther began to cry, while Abigail checked her groans long enough to say: "I've broken my ankle, getting over this horrid wall, and here we are half a mile from home. I shall die; I know I shall; so I might as well have been killed by the bull and done with it. — Oh, this shocking pain!"

"What shall we do?" asked Myrtilla, trying to keep back her tears. She evidently thought that a boy who could face a fierce bull would be capable of helping them.

"I'll run to your house as fast as I can and ask Mr. Seixas to bring a carriage for you."

"No, that will never do. It would frighten my lady to death. She would go into fits, and think somebody had run off with the children."

Isaac reflected a moment, the little girls regarding him with the greatest reverence.

"I have a pony carriage of my own," he said, presently.

"If you can wait here, I'll run and get it for you."

"How do you suppose I can get in a pony

carriage? I can scarcely stir my foot from the ground; and then I've no notion of being drawn like a wild beast through the town for every body to gaze at."

Abigail's sufferings were evidently making her cross. Isaac remained silent, — reflecting how differently his mother would act under the same circumstances, when Esther's tears led him to say:

"You ought to have the Doctor as quickly as possible, or your ancle will be very bad."

"It's *very* bad now!" she said, in a snappish tone.

"Don't be cross, please, nurse," faltered Myrtilla; "Why don't you let the boy go? I love him, he's so kind."

"He may go for all me. I don't know who's hindering him. He might have been half way home by this time."

Isaac was off now on the full run.

"Isn't he good?" questioned Esther, gazing after him.

"I tell you it's the most unfortunate thing that could have happened," groaned Abigail, clasping her hands around the injured ankle. "I never thought to demean myself to accept a favor from a Christian. I despise the whole race of 'em."

The little girls trembled, as they always did when nurse began on this subject, but wisely said nothing.

In less time than they could have expected, they saw Isaac driving toward them at full speed.

"I shall live to rue this day, I know I shall," snarled the woman, spitting toward the lad in token of her contempt. "I wish the bull had killed me, and there would have been an end of it."

"Is she worse?" inquired the boy anxiously. "Mamma was afraid she'd faint with the exertion of getting into the carriage, though it is very low; and she put a bottle of camphor in my pocket. Here it is, holding it out to Myrtilla. Now I'll help you, nurse, the horse is very steady."

"Faint," repeated the woman scornfully. "I never fainted in my life."

But no sooner did she attempt to stand than with a feeble groan she fell back against the wall, the color receding from face and lips.

"Oh, how sick she looks!" screamed Esther, beginning to cry again; "I wish papa was here."

Fortunately at this moment, a countryman driving a pair of oxen came in sight; and to him Isaac applied for help. Abigail, too faint to resist, and really believing that her last hour had come, was lifted into the carriage by the farmer; but as she was too far gone to support herself, Isaac was forced to ride with her head against his shoulder, occasionally wetting his handkerchief with camphor and holding it to her nostrils.

In this way, with the reins of the tame pony between his knees, they walked along the half mile to their home; the twins clasping each other firmly by the hand and following closely behind.

As they approached the principal street, Isaac turned down a lane which would bring them out back of Mr. Seixas's house.

When they reached the gate, Myrtilla ran forward to announce to her father what had happened; and presently the gentleman appeared in a rich cashmere dressing gown faced with crimson silk, a cap, with a tassel of the same hue on his head, and evidently not a little excited by his daughter's hurried account of the accident.

THE JEWISH GIRL RIDING WITH ISAAC.   Page 30.

ASTOR, LENOX AND
TILDEN FOUNDATIONS
R L

CHAPTER III.

PREJUDICED HEARTS.

ISAAC had led the pony close to the lower step and was waiting for help, when Mr. Seixas came forward, his sharp black eyes fixed keenly on the boy's face.

There was a little start and flush of surprise, as if he recognised the youth as the son of his nearest neighbor; but instantly controlling himself, he said to nurse:

"Are you much hurt? Can you bear your weight on your foot?"

Finding her unable to answer distinctly, he sent for the butler, and together they conveyed her to a sofa in the dining hall. Isaac scarcely conscious of what he was doing, following with the basket, containing the scarf which had been the cause of all their trouble.

Meantime Esther had been repeating to her mamma an exaggerated account of the boy's bravery in saving them from the bull, and having an intuitive feeling that she could express their gratitude more kindly than their father, had induced her to go below.

Just as she entered Isaac was bathing Abigail's forehead with the camphor, when to the surprise of all, the lady flew across the room exclaiming with a half sob:

"Who are you, boy? Where did you come from?"

Before he could answer Mr. Seixas appeared at the door having sent a servant for a physician, and quietly led his wife from the room. Then turning to the lad he said:

"From what I hear, you have been very courageous, I cannot thank you now. The excitement has made my wife extremely ill. I am sorry to have to ask you to go, and not to come here again."

Myrtilla pulled his sleeve and whispered something in his ear.

"Yes, child, another time. It is not possible now. He must go at once; but I will see him again."

Casting a lingering, regretful look toward the little girls, without a word the boy took the camphor bottle from the table, and left the house.

Child that he was, it was a great disappointment to him to be dismissed so abruptly.

Mrs. Duncan listened with great interest to his recital of the morning's adventure, and was both surprised and greived that his offices should have met with so poor a return of thanks.

A week passed and not a word from their neighbors. Out of school hours, Isaac could talk of nothing else. Much of his time was passed in his mother's chamber where he could see the twins at play in the garden, and had time to speculate on the condition of the family.

"What could the sick lady mean by asking me such sharp questions? I wonder whether they talk about us. I wonder whether nurse is well."

Every day the doctor's buggy drove up the avenue and stood tied to the iron post for a long time, and almost every day Isaac when he went to post letters for his mother, saw the butler at the apothecary's counter on the same room, waiting for his prescriptions to be made up.

One day near a week after the accident,

the doctor on leaving his new patients drove directly to their own door.

Without giving him time to ring, Isaac flew to the door, when the physician who was their family attendant said:

"So, my lad, you've made quite a hero of yourself. Your'e a brave boy; but where's your mother?

The lady soon entered the parlor.

"I congratulate you, Mrs. Duncan," he began jocosely, on the presence of mind and courage of your son. My patients at the other place can talk of nothing else."

"Who are your patients," she inquired, quietly.

"Both Mrs. Seixas and her nurse, who is rapidly recovering; at least the swelling has abated. It will take a few weeks to knit the bone together."

"Is Mrs. Seixas consumptive?"

"Oh, no! General prostration of the nervous system occasioned by a terrible affliction years ago."

"Which is the cause probably of their desire to seclude themselves?"

"Somewhat so; yes," he answered confusedly. "The fact is, Mr. Seixas is a Jew, and regards Christians with contempt."

"That explains his conduct to me," was the lady's secret thought.

"Isaac looks remarkably well," commented the doctor; growing rapidly! Mrs. Seixas was much struck with his appearance. By the way, I never before noticed how little he resembles you."

He looked her keenly in the face as he said this, but she smiled as she answered:

"We are totally dissimilar. His father, however, was remarkably dark. In that, and in his features, Isaac resembles him."

"Yes! It often happens that a child closely

resembles one parent. Let me see, how old was he when his father died?"

"He was in his fifth year when I took him into the room for a last look. Immediately after that, afflictions came one after another. I lost not only my husband, but a lovely babe, and not being able to endure the painful associations connected with our old home, my brother built this for me near his own."

"Sad loss! sad loss, madam!!" with his eyes still fixed on Isaac. "Very mysterious family! I think the lady has been bereft of her reason at some time; — 'a little weak here now,' — tapping his forhead, — 'natural result, you know, of great excitement,' — 'harps upon her meeting with Isaac continually.' I advise Mr. Seixas to send for the boy; but he objects totally, unless, — Well, I must be going. I still have a dozen patients to call on before I can eat my dinner."

"Is nurse as cross as she was?" eagerly inquired Isaac, starting to his feet, — when the doctor did.

"Yes, yes, her ability in that line is wonderful. She frets at being obliged to accept a favor from the hands of a Christian. The twins are staunch friends though, and do their mother harm by repeating over and over again, your courage in facing the bull, and afterward your kindness to them all. You'll hear from them yet, boy. Mr. Seixas is very reserved, very; but you'll hear in time."

"Can I do any thing for our neighbors in their affliction?" asked Mrs. Duncan, as he turned to go.

"No, I fancy not. Attention or sympathy seem to annoy him. He is wholly devoted to his family and is chagrined that his wife is so excited concerning Isaac. In fact he told me that he would rather have given five hundred dollars than to have had all this happen. The obligation frets him."

Isaac's eyes began to flash. "I wish, doctor, you would tell him that I don't want him to feel any obligation. I did it because I couldn't help it without stopping to think; and I don't want anything for it; nor I shouldn't accept any thing. I like the little girls; but I—"

"Stop! Stop, my dear," murmured his mother softly, laying her hand on his head.

He caught it impulsively, and pressed it to his lips. "Why can't every lady be good like you, mamma," he exclaimed, trying to control himself. "I liked him ever so much at first, till he wouldn't let me."

The lady shook hands with the doctor and then inviting her son to her chamber asked gently: "Will you read a few verses to me Isaac?"

"Yes, mamma! and I can turn to the place at once. He smiled archly as he opened to the thirteenth chapter of the first epistle to the Corinthians.

"Isn't that it," he inquired?

She nodded assent, and he went on.

"Charity suffereth long, and is kind * * is not easily provoked, thinketh no evil * * Charity never faileth."

"I can say it by heart, mamma," he added, when he had finished reading. "I have read it so often. Do you think it would be wicked, though, for me to say that it's mean of him to suppose I want any thing for doing what I did? I am willing he should keep his secrets; and I'm sorry for the sick lady; but 1 hate — I mean, I despise mean people, who can't take a favor when it is kindly meant."

"In that he is no doubt influenced by his prejudiced feelings as a Jew."

"I love Jews," exclaimed the boy. "Christ was a Jew." "Yes, and they are God's chosen people. I love them, too, and pray earnestly for them that their eyes may be opened to behold the true Messiah."

"What makes Jews hate other people so, mamma?"

"There are a number of reasons which I suppose might influence them. I think they always remember that God chose them from all the nations of the earth to be his peculiar people; that to them were committed the sacred books of the law; and that Moses, Joseph, Samuel and all the prophets were Jews."

"I should think they would be more pleased that Jesus was a Jew. I don't see why they hate him so."

"They were, at the time of his coming, greatly oppressed by the Romans under Augustus Cæsar, and they looked for a temporal prince who should deliver them from bondage. When the Saviour came, born in a manger, obliged to flee for his life; so poor that he had not where to lay his head, with only a company of poor, illiterate fishermen for disciples; they would not believe he was the Messiah promised their fathers. They shut their ears to the prophecies so long foretold, and their eyes to the evidence of his miracles and holy life; or, in the words of Isaiah: 'Hear ye, indeed, but understand not; and see ye, indeed, but perceive not.' It was the blessed privilege of the Gentiles then, to receive this precious Saviour, Jesus Christ, the Lord; and to inherit all the promises made to believers.

"The sacrifices and offerings made at the temple for so many years, were all typical of the great sacrifice to be made by him, so that when he was once offered up there was no more need of bulls and of goats to take away sin. Christ, the Lamb of God, had been slain. The old Jewish ceremonies were abolished. The Sabbath was changed from the seventh to the first day of the week; and hereafter all were invited to approach boldly into the presence of their great High Priest, to ask for such things as they might need.

"Do you remember when Pilate remonstrated with the Jews, and offered to give them Barabbas to be crucified, if they would release Jesus? He asked them: 'Why? what evil hath he done?' He said: 'I wash my hands of the blood of this just man.' But they cried out: 'His blood be on us, and on our children.'

"This was the awful curse they brought down on their own heads, which has clung to them ever since. In whatever nation they are found: for it was foretold of them that, for their rejection of Christ, they should be scattered over the world; they are a down-trodden people. Their glory is departed forever. The Lion of the tribe of Judah has now become King of the whole earth."

Isaac's eyes did not once wander from

his mother's face. He sighed heavily as he said:

"I can't help pitying the Jews, mamma."

They used to be great and glorious; and they had such a splendid temple with priests and rabbies at the altar.

"But now there is not left one stone upon another. Do you remember those touching lines I read you?

> 'Our temple hath not left a stone,
> And mockery stands on Salem's throne.'"

"But, mamma, you didn't tell me why Mr. Seixas hates Christians so?"

"I don't pretend to know why *he* hates them; but I said, there were reasons which he might suppose justified such a feeling.

"Perhaps the suspicion that he himself is regarded with the contempt, many feel for the Jews, may prejudice him; or, it may be that he is naturally of an envious, sour temper. There is one thing we can do for him. We can pray; and I feel sure that when you have done so you will no longer be troubled with unkind thoughts of him."

Isaac took up a book but his mother saw by his glances at the house opposite, that his mind was still in that direction. Presently he asked:

"Is there a synagogue in R——, mamma?"

"Oh, yes, my dear!"

"I suppose, then, Mr. Seixas goes to meeting there?"

"Probably, if he goes at all."

"Why don't all Jews go to meeting?"

"I have often noticed, my dear, that they are extremely lax in their religious duties because there is no vitality in them."

"What do you mean, mamma?"

"In whose name, and for whose sake, do we ask blessings?"

"In the name of Christ."

"But they disown, reject, despise him. When they hear his blessed name, they spit in token of their contempt. We have the promise that if we ask in Christ's name we shall receive. They do not ask in his name. It is a mere formal repetition of words, without any vitality or heart; and such prayers cannot be accepted or answered.

CHAPTER IV.

THE CHILD PREACHER.

WEEK after week passed; but Isaac had no opportunity to renew his acquaintance with Myrtilla and Esther. After conversing with his mother on the probability of the twins ever having read the New Testament, or heard of the Saviour, he began to include them in his daily petitions. His heart seemed to be drawn out towards them in a remarkable degree.

One morning while he was at school, Mrs. Duncan stood in the front garden, tying up some flowers, which had fallen from their supports, when she saw a large travelling carriage at her neighbor's door with trunks on behind, indicative of a journey. Presently Mr. Seixas brought out his wife in his arms and placed her within, while a young girl followed with shawls and cushions. There was an affecting adieu to the children who were to be left behind; and then the carriage rolled away.

Ten minutes later a man walked deliberately up the avenue, and seeing her at work, gravely delivered a small package sent, he informed her, by his master, Mr. Seixas.

The lady felt no small curiosity to know what Isaac would say.

"Look on my bureau, my son." The tone was arch and playful.

"Where is it from? and when did it come?"

"This morning, when you were at school."

Hastily he untied the sealed cord, and discovered a beautiful box set with pearls. This contained as she suspected, a watch of exquisite workmanship. The boy examined it in silence, his cheeks flushing.

"It is splendid!" he said at last; "but I had rather he had given me a kind word. I have a watch you know that was father's; and I— I had rather not accept it."

"You had better read your note," she remarked, watching him, much amused. "There it lies at your feet."

He caught it up eagerly, his eyes sparkling. There were but few words which read thus:

"I send a token which I hope may be acceptable, from a grateful father,

JESSE SEIXAS."

A tear-drop sparkled in his eye, as he passed it to his mother, saying: "he might have written more. If he had, I would accept it, now I shall—"

"Do nothing hastily, my son. As he is absent and will probably be so for a long time, you will have an opportunity to reflect what is best. What did you want him to say?"

"I expected he would come some day. He promised to see me again; and that he would tell me I was brave. Every one says that. Then I thought he would ask me to call at his house, where Myrtilla and Esther could tell me how much they loved me."

He laughed as his mother did, when he ended, and then added; "It's foolish for me to think of it; but ever since I knew they were Jews, Iv'e been wanting to — hoping to; I don't mean, convert them; but tell the little girls about the Saviour. It seems so dreadful that they shouldn't know about him."

"It does, indeed. I must confess, Isaac, Iv'e thought a great deal more about them since the doctor told us that. If we could once convince them we are friends, we might gradually gain their confidence. We can at least pray that God would enable us to advance his own work."

"I suppose if I were to return the watch

it would displease him," murmured Isaac thoughtfully.

"I do not know, very likely it might. You must judge on that point for yourself."

Mr. Seixas had been gone two weeks, when on returning from school one afternoon, Abigail saw him from the piazza, and beckoned him to come in.

His heart beat as he obeyed her, and he expressed his joy at seeing her out again.

"You're not as glad as I am," she said;

"I've had a tough time of it. I've been thinking I was not as civil to you as I might have been the day you brought me home."

The boy hastened to assure her that he had forgotten all about her bitter words long ago.

"Well, then, I'm not likely to forget them; for either Myrtilla or Esther are at me continually. Sometimes it is; — 'He's afraid of you, and that is why he never comes to see us;' or else, 'I'm sorry we didn't thank him. Mamma said that we owed him our lives.'"

"Where are the little girls?"

"Wait a minute, and you'll see them coming round the corner, they've found a heap of broken china, and are bringing some choice pieces for their baby house. They're twins you know."

Presently their laugh was heard, and Isaac ran to meet them and help them bring their treasures. He had never had a sister or cousin of an age to be an associate; and he was almost astonished at himself to find how his heart warmed toward those young strangers.

Astonished at his success, and really believing his Heavenly Father had opened the way for him to unfold the sacred truths of the gospel, in ten minutes he was leading the twins up his own avenue for the purpose of obtaining liberty from his mother to return with them for an hour or two.

Mrs. Duncan did her best to please her young visitors who at first were extremely shy, clinging to Isaac as to an old friend.

Over the marble mantle was an exquisitely finished head of the Saviour wearing a crown of thorns. Upon it the eyes of the little girls were fastened; and seeing this, Isaac with a brightly beaming face requested his mother to tell them who it was.

She complied willingly, and with great seriousness of voice and manner asked: "Did you ever see a picture like that before?"

"Yes, ma'am," answered Myrtilla. "In a gallery in Paris."

"Do you know who it is?"

She shook her head.

"It is the Lord; He who came to earth to save us. We call him our Saviour, Jesus Christ."

"He was a dear Jew," added Isaac impulsively. "I love Jews."

"Would you like to hear a story, little girls? If so, come here to-morrow afternoon; and I will tell you a pretty one about a babe who was so poor he had to lie in a manger where the cattle eat."

"We'll come!" was the earnest reply.

"I'm going to ask mamma to let me go to the synagogue some day," said the boy, leading them down the avenue. "Now what shall we play?"

"I like to hear stories best, because I can't read very well," softly answered Esther.

"Well, come into the arbor and I will tell you one. Did you know my uncle used to live here? Yes, he did, and I know all about the place."

Seated in the shade, with the waving boughs casting pleasant shadows all around them, and the birds making sweet music over their heads, Isaac told of the Saviour's mighty works while on the earth: — The miracle of turning water into wine; of raising Lazarus to life; of his love for the sisters of Bethany; of his restoring the blind man to sight; — all these and many more, were rehearsed again and again to his wondering hearers. Nor did he stop until warned by Abigail that the dew was beginning to fall, and that supper-time had long passed. The girl seemed very irritable, and scarcely bid Isaac good bye, as the children clung to him begging him to come again. The boy wondered at the change in her manner toward him, and came to the conclusion that it was a pity the twins had not some one who would be kind to take care of them, little dreaming that she had been an unseen listener to all he had said, and that it was an accusing conscience which made her so cross.

Yes, Abigail for the first time in her life

had heard an account of the Saviour's mission on earth; and the words related with a child's enthusiasm, commented upon freely by her own little charges, had a peculiar fascination in them which carried conviction of their truthfulness to her heart.

True she had at first stolen to a place near the arbor that she might judge what kind of companion he was likely to be for the twins; and true also, that when she first heard the name of the Saviour, she trembled with anger; but after listening awhile, concluded it could do those innocent children no harm to listen to a story of a man of whom they would never be likely to hear again.

Mrs. Duncan was greatly interested in his success, and promised to aid him all in her power. That night both in private and houshold devotions, the whole family of Mr. Seixas was borne in faith to the Mercy-seat, while the richest of heavenly blessings, even a faith to appreciate the beauties of the Saviour's character, was besought for them.

Punctual to the hour, both Myrtilla and Esther were waiting for Isaac at the gate on his return from school. They found Mrs. Duncan had caused a table to be spread under the shade of the great Elm tree on the side lawn, and were delighted to share in the strawberries, cream and cake which she offered them. She then gathered them around her and explained that if our Saviour had not died, we never could have enjoyed the pleasures of this life, but that his love for us was so great that he left heaven where he was reigning with his Father, to come and save us from the consequences of our guilt.

In a brief manner, simple as words could make it, she gave an account of the creation, the fall of man, and the promises made to the father of the faithful that in his seed all the families of the earth should be blessed.

From this time all the rites and ceremonies of the Jews pointed to this Jesus or Saviour who was to come, and the prophets who wrote the books of the Old Testament spoke of him, and what he would do for men. Priests were waiting his coming; men, women and children watched with impatience for him. By and by, he did come, not as they expected with great pomp and splendor like a temporal prince; but as a poor babe in a stable in Bethlehem, one of the small cities of Judea.

CHAPTER V.

PLEADING THE PROMISE.

"MAMMA," inquired Isaac, the color in his dark cheeks coming and going as he listened. "How could they be certain at first that this little babe was the Saviour who had been promised?"

Mrs. Duncan took a small Bible from her pocket and read:

" And there were in the same country, shepards abiding in the fields, keeping watch over their flock by night. And so the angel of the Lord came upon them, and the glory of the Lord shone round about them; and they were sore afraid. And the angel said unto them fear not; for behold I bring you tidings of great joy, which shall be to all people; for unto you is born this day, in the city of David a Saviour, which is Christ the Lord. And this shall be a sign unto you; ye shall find the babe wrapped in swaddling clothes lying in a manger. And suddenly there was with the angel a multitude of the heavenly host praising God and saying: 'Glory to God in the highest; and on earth peace, good will toward men.' And it came to pass, as the angels were gone away from them the shepherds said one to another: Let us now go even unto Bethlehem, and see this thing which has come to pass, which the Lord hath made known unto us. And they came with haste, and found Mary and Joseph and the babe lying in a manger."

When she had finished reading, the lady proposed to the children to have a game of battledoor on the lawn. Isaac found an odd battledoor so that the three could join in the play, and soon the air rung with their merry voices.

They were still playing when Abigail made her appearance walking with some difficulty and told the twins it was time to go home.

Mrs. Duncan offered her a saucer of strawberries; but she declined them rather rudely, and seemed disposed to hurry the children away. But they would not go until they had kissed both Mrs. Duncan and Isaac; and expressed their thanks for her kindness.

What was the astonishment, therefore, of the lad when on passing the gate the next morning, he saw Myrtilla crying as if her heart would break.

"If I'm late at school," said he to himself, "I must find out what is the matter with her," but she could only sob as she told him: "Abigail is ugly and cross, and says;

I must not go to see you and the kind lady again. He cheered her a little by telling her, he himself would plead with Abigail; and then he was obliged to run as fast as he could, to get in before the school room door was locked.

At noon Mrs. Duncun proposed that her son invite nurse to accompany her charge, which had so- good an effect that all three walked up the avenue with him on his return from school. Abigail was pleased that her plan had operated so well, and anxious to hear the particulars of what the twins had been trying to repeat.

Though naturally of a fretful, irritable temper, which she had never been taught to restrain; yet Abigail had a quick perception, a shrewd discriminating mind. Since hearing Isaac in the arbor, her thoughts had constantly reverted to the subject.

" What if the Jews are at fault?" she had

asked herself again and again. "What if Jesus is the promised Messiah? What if their rejection of him has been the cause of their downfall? Look how they used to be greater than all the nations of the earth; their priests walking in splendid robes and a shining breastplate. Now how changed!"

It was with these feelings she accompanied the children to Mrs. Duncan's, hoping, yet fearing that she would pursue the subject.

The lady who had been praying for grace to direct her speech aright, watched the girl closely, and could not but perceive the eagerness which the latter sought to conceal, to hear more of Jesus.

Thinking she could not do better than to impress the truth of the fall and redemption of man upon them, she asked questions upon the stories related the previous day, enlarging upon the subjects where she found they did not understand.

It was not at all her idea to enter with them into any speculative views, of one sect or another, but merely to give them the Bible account of the Saviour, comparing the prophecies of the Old Testament with their fulfilment in the New. She found that in the case of the twins, they had imbibed no prejudices against the name or character of Jesus; and, that their minds seemed peculiarly open to his teachings. They listened with tearful eyes to the account of the mothers, who brought their babes to Jesus that he might bless them, and were indignant with the disciples who rebuked them. They repeated again and again, until they had committed it to memory, the precious words: "Suffer little children to come unto me, and forbid them not for of such is the kingdom of heaven."

With Abigail it was easy to perceive that her mind was filled with bitterness against one, whom from her earliest remembrance she had been taught to believe, was an imposter. As the lady went on talking, or answering the earnest questions of the little ones, her flashing eye, — curled lip, — or dilated nostrils moved, showing that she did not receive all as truth; but the unflagging attention she paid to every word, also indicated that she wished carefully to examine the proofs of Chist's true Messiahship.

Isaac entered into the object of enlightening the minds of these dear Jews, as he called them, with the greatest interest. Occasionally he met Abigail's gaze fixed upon him with a keen scrutiny, and once when his mother was telling of the glory of Solomon's temple with the train of devout worshippers coming and going, from the shambles where they procured their sacrifices of bulls and of goats, the turtle doves and young pigeons, he said:

"Oh, I wish I had been there; I wish I were a Jew!"

"You look like a Jew," was Abigail's quick response.

"Do I really?" querried the boy with a laugh, which was checked instantly, however, as he saw his mother turn pale.

"I fancied the first time I saw you that you looked like Esther," nurse went on; but I suppose it is only because you are so very dark. "I noticed a resemblance," remarked Mrs. Duncun, quietly. "Many brothers and sisters look less alike;" and then she proceeded with her account of the temple.

When she thought she had told them as much as they could remember, urging them in her sweet, winning way, to love this Saviour who had done so much for them, she said to Abigail: "I suppose you can understand something of Hebrew; most Jews can."

"No, ma'am," was the hesitating reply. "Mr. Seixas reads in Hebrew as well as in English."

"It is a glorious language, — the language in which the Old Testament was written. I can chant a little; would you like to hear a verse which the poor Jews chant?"

"Oh, indeed, we should!"

"Well, then, we may suppose them to be sitting by the stream with their harps hung on the willows, making their mournful lament."

She chanted in Hebrew, and then translated for them the following touching stanza;

> "But we must wander witheringly,
>   In other lands to die;
> And where our father's ashes be,
>   Our own must never lie;
> Our temple hath not left a stone,
>   And mockery stands on Salem's throne."

"We ought to thank you, ma'am," said Abigail, really making an effort to conceal the tears which filled her eyes: "but I'm beginning to be afraid. Master will be displeased at my coming here. He's not very strict to be sure, for before the sad affliction that changed them all, I've heard mistress say that he went as much with Gentiles as with Jews. Mistress often begs him to take her to the Synagogue; but he seldom cares to go. Her going is out of the question; though, poor lady, she fancies she might get comfort there."

Mrs. Duncan longed to inquire to what affliction the woman referred, but disliked to question a servant of what concerned her master's family. She bade them an affectionate adieu, and then sat reflecting on the probability that Mr. Seixas would forbid their receiving instruction from her when he returned.

From what Abigail said, her mistress still suffered from the afflictive event, whatever it was, and was vainly seeking comfort where it could not be found. Mrs. Duncan's whole heart was moved with compassion for the poor invalid and retiring to her closet she committed her to the mercy of a loving Saviour who longs to embrace her as a child.

She entreated the Holy Spirit to enlighten the dark minds of those, who living in the full blaze of religious light and liberty, still groped in darkness, waiting in vain for a deliverer yet to come, — that their eyes might be opened to see in Jesus the Prince of Peace promised to Abraham, to Isaac and to Jacob, — the Lion of the tribe of Judah, — that they might accept him as their Saviour and thus be delivered from the terrible curse their father had entailed.

CHAPTER VI.

MYSTERY INCREASING.

AFTER two days of rainy weather, Isaac became so impatient for a sight of his little friends, that with his mother's permission he ran to the door to inquire for them.

The butler answered the summons, and replied that he would call Abigail.

The girl's face flushed crimson when she saw who it was, and quickly shutting the door behind her to prevent his hearing a cry from Myrtilla, she answered in the old cross tone:

"The twins are at their lessons, and can't be disturbed. Master is coming home to-morrow, and so the visiting must all be done with."

"Can't I see them one minute then," urged the boy earnestly; "Just to say good bye."

"No, you can't," and without another word she shut the door in his face.

It required a great effort for the lad, twelve years old though he was, to keep back his tears. He walked quickly up the avenue and rushed into his mother's chamber, sure of meeting her sympathy.

"It is God's work, my child, that we have undertaken, and we can leave it with him. I am truly sorry for you, and for the sweet children who, I think, will be equally disappointed with yourself; but perhaps it will not be so long a separation as you fear; perhaps they will persuade their father to allow them to come."

"May I carry a bouquet to Mrs. Seixas in the morning, mamma?"

"Yes, dear."

"I will gather it early while the dew is on the flowers, and hang them to the knob of the door."

This he did with a card attached by a white ribbon, on which were the simple words:

"Welcome home, dear lady.

Isaac."

Little did the boy or his mother imagine when he wrote, and she applauded the neatness of the penmanship, that this small expression of his interest and affection, would plunge the invalid into the depths of woe, — that the sight of these flowers, so tastefully arranged, would more than undo all the benefit she had received from her journey; that even the name at the bottom would cause a flood of sad memories, which would threaten to destroy her reason, if not her life.

Yet it was so; though not until weeks after did he learn the sad result.

Poor fellow! how he waited and watched for some answer to his short epistle; " I would be satisfied with only one tiny flower," he said to his mother, "just to show that she was pleased." How little he dreamed of the wrath of Mr. Seixas at finding all his cautions disregarded; that Abigail herself had conveyed the flowers to her mistress, and that in consequence, a perfect torrent of vile epithets was coupled with his name.

At last his faith began to fail; for, had he not prayed earnestly, believing that he should be heard; and yet, had not God shut the door against any further efforts in his behalf?

" We must be willing to wait God's time, Isaac. You remember the promise came to Abraham; but long years did his children wait before the Messiah came; before the set time for their deliverance."

" But, mamma, if I only knew that the little girls had not forgotten about Jesus. They are so very young, only seven, you know, and they had never heard of him before."

"Perhaps for that very reason the account of his sufferings and death, may make an impression. Certainly, Abigail is old enough; and, if I do not mistake, began to ask herself, 'Is not this the Christ?'"

"I'm afraid Mrs. Seixas is ill again," said Mrs. Duncan, meeting Abigail a few days after their return. "I see the doctor makes very frequent visits there."

"She has never been worse," was the reply, in a tone which precluded farther inquiry.

"And the little girls, are they well?"

"Tolerably so."

She repeated the questions, and her replies to her master to show him how reserved she had been, when to her astonishment, he burst out into a fury of rage, and cursed the day when he came to the place; cursed the hour when that boy was born, who, with his dark locks and fatal name, ever brought the dreary past fresh before them.

"I will sell again and go back to Europe; or I will return to New Orleans," he exclaimed, flushed with passion.

"It can't be worse there than here. That boy with his Jewish face will drive us all mad."

It was difficult for Isaac to fix his mind on his lessons. Even his mother did not imagine what yearnings of heart disturbed his thoughts by day and his dreams by night. At last he began to look thin and sallow, and as vacation was approaching she determined to engage a friend to keep house for her, and take a journey to the springs.

Early in August, then, they engaged a carriage to take them to the depot, not at all conscious with how much relief and delight their departure was regarded by their neighbors.

After an absence of nearly two months, they returned each invigorated by the change of air and scene, and also delighted to be at home again.

John came to the depot to meet them, and had scarcely waited for them to be seated in the carryall before he turned back, saying:

"There's great news for ye ma'am. It's true as I always prophesied, that there's no good in them Jews. Mr. Seixas is carried off to prison for a thief; and they do say Abigail as you call her, has got sick of being a Jew, and has turned Christian."

"How dreadful!" exclaimed Isaac; "I don't believe he is a thief."

"That concerning the woman is, indeed, good news," said the lady, a throb of gratitude swelling her heart as she thought perhaps her feeble words had been blessed. "But how did you hear all this, John?"

"'The town is full of it ma'am; and they say Mrs. Seixas is well nigh distracted. There's more stories, too, casting a glance at the distressed countenance of Isaac; but I can't say as how they're true."

"When did this happen?"

"Yesterday week, ma'am."

When they drove to their own door, the doctor was just alighting from his gig; and scarcely had Mrs. Duncan laid aside her outer garments, before he rang and asked to see her.

"We're all in a state of excitement here, ma'am," he began abruptly; "I presume you've heard of the sad event. I can't say, but I've had my suspicions; Mrs. Seixas is in a sad state, though more sane than usual. She persists in asserting that her husband is arrested by mistake. Not very likely," he added, with an incredulous smile.

"Can I be of service in any way, doctor?"

"Why, yes; I came in to ask you to visit the lady. The nurse has been on the watch for you. A great change there; and by the way, Isaac had better not show himself at the other house for the present.

"For what reason, doctor?" she asked in surprise.

"Because, Mrs. Seixas is only just recovering from the effect of receiving a bouquet from him; if you had been at home I should have explained some circumstances connected with him; but I have not time now."

"Only one thing, doctor," asked the lady, growing white.

"Has Isaac done any thing wrong, to cause this dislike; or is it mere prejudice?"

"Dislike; prejudice, bless me! Why how you talk! Mrs. Seixas, if she could have her way, would have him in her arms in a minute, from his resemblance to her son."

She sat down. And indeed, she looked as if she was about to faint; but almost instantly controlling herself, said: "You surprise me more and more; Mr. Seixas has always repelled him; sometimes rudely."

"Because it throws her into convulsions; that's all! He watches him from behind the curtain by the hour."

She saw that he was regarding her with close scrutiny and rising with difficulty said: "I will take some refreshment and go at once."

Ringing the bell, she ordered a cup of tea and some toast with a slice of ham to be brought to her room; and then retiring to her closet, she prayed for grace to do right whatever sacrifice might be demanded of her.

Then having eaten, and dashed cold water repeatedly on her throbbing temples, she went out to find Isaac.

"The doctor has been for me to go to Mr. Seixas's," she said, trying to speak cheerfully. I want to ask you not to leave the house until I return." Then kissing his forehead she left him.

CHAPTER VII.

FROM PALACE TO PRISON.

ABIGAIL was at the window, and without waiting for her to ring, ran down to open the door.

"Ye've come to a sad house, ma'am; but I've been longing for ye. Mrs. Seixas is not like her husband, and since he went I've been trying to comfort her with some of the words you told the children; but it's little I know myself."

The girls face grew very red as she spoke, but Mrs. Duncan took her hand gently and said:

"Is it true, Abigail, that you have begun

to love Jesus and take him for your Saviour?"

"Yes, I have, ma'am; if he'll take me, after all I've done to throw contempt on him.

"The lady at your house lent me Master Isaac's Bible, no offence I hope? and I read it all over and over what he said and did. I see it now as I never did before; and oh, it's such a comfort to know he'll be my friend.

"I could talk forever, ma'am, but mistress needs me."

"I hope I shall have an opportunity to talk with you again."

The girl looked pleased, but led the way softly up the stairs to her mistress' darkened room.

Mrs. Seixas, pale and wan, was sitting up in a lounging chair supported by pillows, the covers trimmed with the most exquisite lace, and every thing about the room betokening not only wealth but refined taste.

She smiled feebly as Mrs. Duncan took her hand saying in an apologizing tone:

"Excuse my rising; I am very weak.

"Abigail bring a chair near me for the lady, and then leave us alone."

"The twins are very impatient to see her, ma'am, might I bring them in for a minute?"

"Yes."

She looked wearied already, and had recourse to a bottle of cologne standing on a teapoy near her.

"I'm afraid you'll think us very intrusive," she said feebly, "but the children talk so much of you"— She checked herself as if approaching a forbidden subject, and then added with a little confusion, "I am separated from all my friends. I need a friend, and Abigail told me you would be one. She says you do not despise us because we are Jews."

"On the contrary, I love the Jews; and I have reason to love them. My husband's life was once saved by a Jew who jumped from the boat and swam to his assistance."

Here she was interrupted by a soft hand stealing into her's, and presently both Myrtilla and Esther pressed foward for a kiss.

Their mother smiled, but seemed relieved when a moment after, nurse urged them to return to their play. They had evidently been forbidden to speak of Isaac, for when Esther began to say: " Where is " — Abigail checked her by a quick gesture.

The instant the door was closed the sick lady, with the impatience of a child, began:

" May I tell you all about it?"

" Yes, every thing."

" Years ago, Jesse's brother, — they are twins, — committed a dreadful sin. It was not exactly stealing, and yet — it was worse. They were travelling together, he and the sick gentleman; the invalid died suddenly in the night, leaving all his concerns in the hands of Justin. The temptation was too much for him; he was not rich, nor good like his brother; and he determined to forge a will and keep all the dead man's money."

"I'm afraid this will excite you," urged Mrs. Duncan, as she saw how often the cologne was in requisition.

"I must tell you. I can rest afterward and take opium. I'm obliged to take it often now; but to go on. We were in New Orleans at that time, boarding at the St. Charles; but we knew nothing of all this, until one day Justin met his brother in the street and followed him home. Never did twins so nearly resemble each other. It was only by their voices that I knew them apart. The landlord and the boarders were constantly addressing Justin as my husband, which caused many a joke. Jesse wondered how his brother came by so much money, who at last explained that he had become heir to a great fortune; and that he was going to travel in Europe. My husband urged and urged to see the will, and at last Justin showed it to him.

"I can see them at this minute; Jesse sitting with the paper in his hand, looking at the signature through a glass, and Justin scowling behind his chair.

"It is forged," my husband said. "Oh! it makes me tremble now, to think what a scene there was then. You wouldn't wonder I'm such a wreck if you knew all. Jesse insisted that his brother had written the name at the bottom of the will, and Justin swore that he did not. But he grew pale and then angry. Oh, so angry! But when Jesse told him he must restore the money to the rightful heirs, or he would expose him, the wicked man swore with a horrid oath that if he dared do it, he would take such revenge that we should remember it to the last day of our life.

"And we have. Yes, yes! Oh, why didn't

we think what he would do and prevent it? Why didn't we flee from him with our best, our dearest treasure!"

The last words were uttered with almost a shriek.

Mrs. Duncan rose instantly, and summoning Abigail, asked for some ammonia, and administered half a tea spoonful. It was near an hour before the poor creature spoke again; but she kept hold of Mrs. Duncan's hand, and seemed so afraid she would leave her, that the lady soothed her by saying:

"Try and take a little wine and water. I am in no hurry, and will stay by you."

"I shall feel better when I have told the worst. We had a darling child five years old. I loved him, I idolized him. I thought of nothing but my husband and my son. Justin knew where to strike to wound us most deeply. One day I went out to ride, leaving the boy with his nurse. When we returned he was gone, — stolen. Justin had taken him, pretending to be his father, and saying that I wished him to ride with us. The girl unable to distinguish between her master and his brother, thought nothing of it, dressed him and let him go.

"I was near my confinement, and was immediately seized with spasms. I lost my reason, too, and knew nothing rightly until Myrtilla and Esther were four months old. My husband has spent a fortune searching for his brother; but I have never seen my sweet little Isaac since."

Mrs. Duncan started and turned as white as the lady on the bed.

"Isaac! Was his name Isaac?" she gasped, trembling in every limb.

"Yes, and I never can hear the name without a pang. You know, or perhaps you can imagine, how I felt when your boy sent me the flowers, and I saw the name *Isaac* there."

Mrs. Duncan rose with difficulty and went to the window.

"Can it be," she asked herself, "that Isaac, — but no, the name is unlike. Seaton was the man who? — Seixas! no; the idea is foolish. Why can't I be calm? Hearing this poor lady's story has strangely moved me. And yet it was in New Orleans I met him; and Isaac was five years old. Oh, if it should prove that my boy is the Isaac she mourns; how can I give him up?"

Here she began to breathe so quickly, that merely saying: "excuse me a moment," she went below.

"I do not feel well," she said to Abigail; "I will go to the parlor for a moment."

"Shall I bring you a cordial, ma'am? You look sick."

"A little water only."

She entered the parlor listlessly, and sank heavily into a chair; but presently started forward as her eyes caught a glimpse of a portrait hanging from the walls.

"Mr. Seaton!" she ejaculated; "but how came he here?"

"It is my master's portrait, ma'am," explained Abigail, coming in with the ice water on a salver.

"And his twin brother," faltered the lady; "Is this his portrait too?"

"I have heard mistress say they couldn't be told apart."

"God help me, then! It must be true!"

Mrs. Seixas was greatly distressed when told by nurse that her visitor was taken suddenly ill in the parlor, and was obliged to go home.

Abigail had her own suspicions, too, which she determined not to impart to her mistress, but contented herself for the rest of the day in longing for her master to return.

The next morning she took Mr. Powers into

her confidence, the secret having magnified itself to such importance.

"Something's going to happen," she began, mysteriously. "It's my opinion that nature is a great institution. Nature told Mrs. Seixas, Isaac was her lost boy, and I believe he is!"

She then repeated the facts upon which her suspicions were founded, ending with, and "I believe that Mrs. Duncan married the rascal who stole the little boy, and that's how she came to have him."

In the morning the doctor came and found his patient extremely low, with a quick, wiry pulse, and a hectic flush on her cheek.

Thoughts of a consultation with some eminent physician crossed his mind; but when he proposed it to her, she shook her head, saying:

"It is hard to minister to a mind diseased. Give me back my husband and my son, and I shall be well. I have tried to convince myself that Isaac was dead. It would be better so than that he should be suffering; but he is not dead; I saw him last night in my dreams. He stood by me and called me: 'mamma, dear lady;' and then he asked: 'Did you get my flowers?' Yes, I'm sure he's living."

She put her hands to her temples to stop their wild beating; and it was as much as Abigail could do not to impart some hope that she would soon see her long lost child. Going down the stairs with the doctor, she put her fingers to her lips murmuring:

"Something's going to happen. Mrs. Duncan could tell you if she chose."

"Ah! Mrs. Duncan! She is ill, I hear. At any rate she sent for me. Have you heard any thing from your master?"

"Not a word; but here is Powers with letters."

"I'm sent for," said the man; "I'm to take the night train and reach New York to-morrow noon."

"There'll be great news for ye to carry, or I'm mistaken," said Abigail, in her old curt tone.

CHAPTER VIII.

FROM HOME TO HOME.

"I NEED your advice, doctor," exclaimed Mrs. Duncan, advancing quickly toward him.

"You look feverish."

"It is not in body, but in mind, that I am ill; but sit down; I hope you are not in haste."

The doctor thought of two patients sick with fever, and one boy taken in a fit the night before; but he said: "no, not specially." He was curious to hear what Mrs. Duncan could tell if she chose.

"Call to mind if you please the conversation

we had once concerning Isaac, and I said his father was very dark and that the boy closely resembled him. If Isaac had not been present I may or I may not have told you, that his father as I took the man to be, was not my husband."

"Mrs. Duncan! Do I understand you aright?"

"Do not judge me yet. I had a husband, a noble Christian man. We lived most happily together; but we had one trial, we had no child. We often spoke of adopting a boy; and one day a man to whom my husband supposed himself to be under the greatest obligations, but who I now think was only his twin brother, came and begged us to adopt his son, a little Jewish boy five years old."

"Exactly!" said the doctor clapping his hands; "but what of the last farewell?"

"That it was precisely as I told you. Mr. Seaton, as the gentleman called himself, told us that for certain reasons which he satisfactorily explained, he wished to leave the country immediately; indeed his passage was already engaged on board a vessel bound for Havre; he said that he had intended to carry Isaac with him but that the boy grieved so much for his mother, who had recently died that he had concluded not to hazard his life, by taking him a long journey without any female attendant. He was to be on board ship by dawn, and thought best to take leave of his son over night.

"I myself took the boy to the chamber telling him he was to see his father. He was overjoyed, and clung so convulsively to the man's neck, beseeching to be carried back to mamma, dear mamma, that I never doubted for an instant that his statements were true. The next morning we also left New Orleans for our home, where I soon forgot all these scenes by the dreadful affliction that came upon me. My husband died; and, during the dark season that followed, my greatest comfort was that lovely boy. He has been my blessing ever since; and how I can bear to part with him I cannot tell."

"Wonderful! truly wonderful!!" murmured the doctor trying to conceal his emotions. Sometime you must tell me how you came to find out that Mr. Seaton was not his father, though as I have heard Mrs. Seixas's story, I can readily guess. Now I think before any thing else, we owe a duty to that poor man who is languishing in prison for his brother's crime; and it just occurs to me that you can be an important witness for him. You who had seen this Mr. Seixas, and were deceived into supposing the other gentleman to be the one."

"No, I never saw him. At least, I don't know that I have. My husband with a party of friends went out in a sail boat on the gulf, and there his life was saved by a gentleman who was then in another boat. Afterwards he came to see Mr. Duncan while he was suffering from the effects of the accident. Then my husband informed me that he urged the man to give him an opportunity to return the obligation. The circumstances I have related followed almost immediately, certainly in a day or two.

"Justin must have heard of the event, and meanly determined to take advantage of it."

The doctor made a motion to go, when she detained him.

"Only one thing more," she said. "By never referring to these incidents in his early history, I have hoped that Isaac would forget them. I firmly believe that he considers me his own mother. How little I thought that the unusual interest he has taken in this family was the natural yearning of his heart for his real parents!"

The physician walked to the bookcase where for five minutes he appeared deliberately studying the name of every volume, but turning abruptly, he said: "I believe after all I had better go with Powers to the city to-night.

"I must tell the poor mother first a fact which will be better than medicine to her, after which I can leave her with you and Isaac."

"I am afraid I can benefit her but little. You forget that what is her gain, will be my loss."

"Isaac will never forget you, ma'am."

"My only comfort is that by his means, God may convert the whole family to Christ."

"True! The father is only half a Jew; his mother was a Greek. Mrs. Seixas is a full-blooded Israelite, a daughter of the celebrated Rabbi, — but really I must be going."

There was one duty Mrs. Duncan was unwilling any one but herself should perform, and that was to tell Isaac that he was her son only by adoption. This was a most painful duty; and no sooner did the doctor take his leave than she sought strength from above to perform it aright. As he might be sent for at any moment, there could be no delay, and therefore, ringing the bell she asked the servant to find him and say, she wished to see him.

"Are you better, mamma?" he asked.

"I cannot think of myself, my dear son," she answered, taking his hand and gazing tenderly in his face, "at least not of my bodily health. I am thinking of you, and how delighted I was when a kind Providence placed you in my arms. Do you remember any thing about your very early life? I mean before we came here."

"Sometimes I think of things which seem to have happened; and then I consider them as dreams."

"What things?"

He grew very red as he replied: "Since Mr. Seixas's family have come, I have thought more about them. I think it must have been a dream, that somebody told me once I was a Jew."

"And would you be pleased if that were the case? I mean of course a Jew by birth; but not a Jew in rejecting the Saviour."

"Oh, I never could be that, but I should like to be of the same nation that he was!"

"What would you think if I were to tell you that you are not only a Jew, but the lost son of Mr. Seixas,—the loss of whom has made the poor mother the sad invalid that she has been for years?"

Isaac tried to smile; but there was a white streak about his mouth.

"How can that be?" he asked, seizing her hand and kissing it passionately. The action gave her strength to go on, and she repeated to him the story she had told the doctor, his head meanwhile sinking lower and lower until with a cry he burst into tears.

"Then the curse is on me," he said vehemently. "I who love the Saviour so, must bear it alway. I did not think I should ever really be a Jew. I can't be any body's boy but yours."

She clasped him to her heart and wept bitter tears, as she thought of the separation which was so close at hand; but even then, she was trying to think how she could comfort him.

They were interrupted by a childish voice at the door, saying:

"Where is Isaac, my brother Isaac? Where is he?"

He hid his head on her shoulder, as if he dreaded the coming interview.

"You love the twins," she said softly.

"Yes; but not as I do you. I loved Mr.

Seixas in spite of all his crossness; but I, — oh, I can't have him for a father. I can't leave you!"

"God has a great work for you to do there, Isaac. Think how you can talk with the little girls about the Saviour; and the mother will listen to any thing from the lips of one raised, as it were, from the dead. It is a great, a terrible trial to me, my darling boy; but God will give me strength to bear it. You will always be a son to me."

"Isaac, Isaac," cried a voice in the hall; "a little girl is calling for you."

"Let her come up here," he said; and throwing himself into a chair, he buried his face in his hands.

"Precious child!" faltered the lady, opening the door. Myrtilla rushed up to her brother, her face covered with smiles, exclaiming: "Isaac, you are to be my real brother now Mamma is waiting to see you. Come!"

"You had better go, my dear," urged Mrs. Duncan.

"I shall come back then?"

"Certainly."

But he did not come. The mother covetous of her new treasure, would not part with it for a moment; and Mrs. Duncan, after waiting for him until a late hour, retired for the first time in seven years without praying by the bedside of her boy.

The next morning she had time to realize how much he had added to the interest of her every day life, and to feel how lonely she would be when he was permanently located at a distance. Her tears fell thick and fast upon the sacred page, as, sitting in her customary seat in the parlor, she read the holy book and entreated God's blessing upon the duties of the day. Earnest petitions ascended for him, but he was not there to join in them, nor to give her an affectionate kiss when they arose.

At breakfast a plate was placed for him and a chair set as usual; but it was vacant, and the consequence was that the lady arose from the table after a mere form of eating.

"I cannot endure this," she said at length. "I must have some object in life. How little I appreciated the blessing of a child, — a warm, loving nature — while it was mine."

Then her thoughts recurred to the situation of Mr. Seixas, in his confinement, all unconscious of the joy in store for him; and she offered a silent prayer that the favor of God to him might soften his proud heart, and bring it into subjection to the Prince of Peace.

CHAPTER IX.

SAD, YET REJOICING.

"IN the mean time, where was Isaac?"

If his mamma, as he still called Mrs. Duncan, could have looked into that front chamber and heard what was said there, I think she would have been comforted in her loneliness, and have offered up fervent thanksgiving that the seed sown with such care in the mind of her boy, watered by her constant prayers, was yielding fruit to the glory of God.

Mrs. Seixas, sitting in her lounging chair, her eye beaming with an expression of happiness foreign to it for many a year, is clasping the hand of Isaac, who occupies a tabouret drawn close to her side. Myrtilla and Esther are on the floor at their feet, while Abigail, as she moves gently about the room in the performance of her morning tasks, often turns aside to brush away a tear as she listens to Isaac's earnest words.

Look at him now! He has forgotten that within twenty-four hours he has grown rich in the possession of father, mother and sisters. See his eye light up, and then grow dim, as he tells these new found relatives of the love of Jesus Christ, the babe of Bethlehem, son of David's line, whom David in prophetic vision called "the Lord's annointed;" whom Moses, the great law-giver of Israel, styled a prophet, whom the Lord our God should raise up like unto himself.

Listen to his earnest voice as he says: "Jesus Christ, the Lord of heaven and earth, is my friend, — my brother. I feel nearer than ever to him now that I know I am a Jew. I feel sure that he loves me, too; that he is praying his Father in heaven for me. Wont you love him too, mother? Wont you believe that he is the Messiah promised for the redemption of Israel?"

"I will do any thing, my son, to please you; but you ask an impossibility when you wish me to become a believer in an impostor. Why, Isaac, my precious child, do you believe that Jehovah would have consented that his son, as Jesus calls himself, should have demeaned himself to work at a carpenter's bench? You say that he was born in a manger. Why if he had been the Messiah so long waited for, the splendor attending the birth of a great Prince would have been nothing compared to his coming?"

Instead of answering, Isaac laid his head on his mother's shoulder and burst into tears.

Startled by this unexpected emotion, Mrs. Seixas turned pale when Myrtilla who had only understood that her brother loved the Saviour and wanted them all to love him, exclaimed earnestly:

"I do love Jesus, and I prayed to him as the lady told me; and then I dreamed that he took my hand and said the sweet verse:

'Suffer little children to come unto me.'

Hav'nt I remembered it well?"

"I can't explain, as mamma does," faltered the boy, trying to check his sobs. "I never understood till now why she always talked with me so much about the Jews and made me love them, and showed me how the prophecies regarding the Messiah were all fulfilled in him. Why don't you remember how David said that they should part his garments among them, and for his vesture they should cast lots; and it was exactly so. The wicked men who crucified the Saviour came along, and stuck a spear into the two thieves, and were going to do the same to

Jesus; but they found he was dead already, so they divided his clothes; but the vesture or the loose robe that he wore had no seam in it, being woven entire. So they cast lots for that."

"It might happen so. I would like to believe for your sake, but my father, who was one of the most learned Rabbies among the Greeks, explained all these things to me. It was common to divide the clothes among the executioners; and of course if the vesture was without seam, they would not render it worthless by tearing it in two; they would prefer to run their chance of getting it whole."

"Dear mother," murmured Isaac, his eyes heavy with tears; "I hope you will not be like the people, the prophet Isaiah tells us about, who having ears hear not and having eyes see not, I can't convince you myself that Jesus is really God; but I can pray to the Holy Spirit to help you to see it."

"Mistress tells me," urged the Jewish nurse, " that she never knew me to be so light-hearted; and indeed, I was a burden to myself while I was groping my way in the dark, as it were, scarcely daring to shut my eyes lest God should come in wrath; for I knew that I had committed many sins and no sin offering had made me whole. But when I heard that Jesus was the great sacrifice and that I might go to God with him in my arms, as the Jews of old carried their lambs to the altar, a mountain's weight was rolled off me. I had found what I wanted; a friend high enough to talk with God for me; and low enough to hear my voice. Since that the night seems like morning to me, and my heart is full of singing."

Isaac rose, saying: " I will go now and see mamma. She has but me, you know; and she will wonder why I don't go for my morning kiss."

"Send for her to come here. Don't leave me," urged the mother piteously; at least not till your father comes. She is kind, I am sure she will come to us here."

"Isaac hesitated. The pale grief-worn face looked very wistfully into his, but in truth he longed for a good hearty cry, such as in years gone by, he used to have to give vent to his over-excited feelings, with his head laid in his dear mamma's lap.

"Shall I go, or stay?" was the question he was asking himself, when a servant came bringing a letter to his mother from her husband.

"Sit by me while I read what your father says. It is not what his next letter will be, full of joy that his son is found at last. Myrtilla, you and Esther may run over and ask Mrs. Duncan to come and spend the morning with us."

Not being accustomed to any reserve in

their own family circle, the lady tore off the envelope and commenced reading the letter aloud.

It was full of rejoicing that the detectives had at last traced the real culprit to Baltimore, and equally full of vengeance toward his brother for having pursued him to the death.

"'Eye for eye and tooth for tooth,'" muttered Abigail; "Now, Isaac, what would Jesus say to that?"

"He would say; 'love your enemies; bless them that curse you; pray for them that despitefully use you and persecute you.'"

"That would not be possible. It is contrary to nature."

In the closing paragraph Mr. Seixas said; "If the boy who lives opposite continues to give you annoyance, let the doctor give notice to his mother. If that does not succeed we must use harsher measures."

Poor Isaac hid his face by gazing from the

window. He saw Mrs. Duncan in her chamber and his heart bounded toward her. Never, never before, had he realized what a blessing she had been to him.

The house, too, with the woodbine clinging so lovingly to the pillars, seemed the abode of peace and harmony.

Now Mrs. Duncan sees him; and bows with a smile. He can resist no longer; but with a bound is down the stairs, across the street, up the avenue, in her dear arms.

"I never, *never* loved you so dearly as now," he murmured, checking a sob. "I never knew how much I owed you."

Myrtilla stood by, wondering to see her pass her hand caressingly over his forehead; a sweet, placid smile resting on her countenance.

"I was just going over to see you, my child," she said tenderly. "Myrtilla says her mamma wants you near her all the time."

"I want to see you a little while first. Myrtilla can tell her I'll be there soon."

He sat down in his old seat; but instead of talking took her hand and put it on his head.

"It aches," he said presently; and after a few moments added, "and so does my heart."

Gently she soothed him while he told her of his sorrow that he could not persuade his mother to receive the Saviour.

"I never, *never* can bear it," he exclaimed vehemently.

"Don't be discouraged, my dear. It is not easy to clear away the prejudices of a whole life-time in a single hour. You have tried to convince her that Jesus was the promised Messiah; now I advise you to let her see by your life what his love can do. Pray for her and all your new relatives. Pray earnestly, remembering the promise to those who ask. Think what happiness to become God's instrument in bringing them to the Saviour."

"Do you know that Mr. Seixas—my father, I mean, has written about me? He calls me, 'That boy.' Are you very sure, mamma, that I am his child? Perhaps there is some mistake yet; then we will forget all about this. I mean I will forget that I am not your real, own boy; and we will be so happy, as we were before."

"I am afraid it is too true, Isaac. I say *afraid*, because whatever the change may be to you, to me it is a sad, sad affliction."

"Do you think he will ever cease to be a Jew, mamma?"

"I hope not," with emphasis; "but I hope he will embrace Jesus, as the Messiah promised to Abraham, to Isaac and to Jacob. Then will he be a Jew, or an Israelite, in the truest sense of the word."

"But if it is so hard to convince her, it will be almost impossible to make him believe."

"Nothing is impossible with God. His

grace can convert the most obdurate heart. Let him see you cheerful, obedient, truthful; and let him learn that you are all these out of regard to your Saviour, and he will begin to inquire what is the principle, which caused such happy results? What is the fountain from which such pleasant streams are flowing?"

"I wish I could, mamma; but you always told me my great danger was in my quick, fiery temper. Now when I am away from you, I don't know how I shall govern myself. If he calls me 'that boy,'" Isaac's eye flashed, "or if he treats me harshly, I'm afraid I shall grow angry."

"I think there is far more danger of your receiving too much indulgence; that you will be praised and petted," she answered, smiling at his vehemence; but if it ever should be as you have imagined, the motive of leading, winning him to your Saviour, would I hope, be strong enough to lead you to restrain your wrath."

You must always remember that you need not depend on yourself for strength; that you can have help from above by simply asking for it."

" I wonder when he will come home? They have goten a trace of the real criminal. Mother says that ever since that first crime, my uncle has been growing worse and worse; they often heard of him while they were in Europe, and twice father, (how strange it seems to say that name,) was greatly annoyed by being mistaken for him. She thinks father will not be at liberty until he is taken, and has his trial."

They heard a sound of little steps up the avenue, and presently Esther ran in exclaiming:

" You have been gone a long time, Isaac, mamma can't wait any longer."

The boy arose, saying; " You will come, mamma," and went with her down the stairs.

" I was afraid it was all a dream," said the lady, apologizing, as Mrs. Duncan entered.

" She was getting as nervous as a witch, ma'am," interrupted Abigail.

CHAPTER X.

HOME FROM PRISON.

THE fact of Dr. Strong's being absent from his patients three consecutive days was an event unheard of in the annals of the town. The young physician in whose hands he had left his patients, was to be sure unwearied in his attentions; but there was great anxiety to know what had become of the old doctor.

On the morning of the fourth day quite a band of villagers were collected around the depot, curious to learn whether he would arrive in that train; but he did not.

An hour later, however, a carriage drove rapidly up to Mr. Seixas's door, and Isaac who was sitting near the window with his mother, saw his father and the doctor alight.

"It's your husband," he said, his face flushing crimson.

"And your father! How rejoiced he will be!"

They had no time for another word before the door opened; quick steps bounded up the stairs and the lost child was fervently clasped in his father's arms.

All the speculations upon the manner of his reception, the dread of coldness, the nameless anxieties as to the meeting, were forgotten in that long embrace.

At last wondering that he did not speak, Isaac glanced into his father's face. He saw that the strong man was moved to his very depths; the quivering chin, the moistened eyes, the heaving breast, all betokened the struggle necessary to maintain self-control.

Mrs. Duncan sat weeping unconsciously as

she watched them; but her's were tears which brought relief.

"The Lord be praised!" was the fervent ejaculation which escaped from his lips. "My son, more precious than a mine of gold, have you no word for your father?"

"Love me please, dear father."

"Love you! My heart is swelled with love; the love crushed back for seven years, till it is almost bursting."

"I will try to be a good son."

"He is a good son;" faltered the mother. "I shall be well now. Isaac restored to us we need no longer fear what Justin can do. Oh, we shall be so happy!"

"Ah!" murmured the gentleman, with a shade of anguish; "his soul has gone back to his Maker."

Then shaking off with an effort the gloomy thoughts natural to such a subject, he drew a chair near his wife's, and said:

"Sophia, you look ten years younger than when I left you. Joy is a great beautifier. Well, my son, you can understand now, why the sight of your genuine Jewish face gave us all so much pain."

"I can only partly understand it."

"Let me explain, then, for it is fit that in this hour of happy re-union, all should be understood."

"Papa has come! papa! papa!" echoed happy voices on the stairs.

He sprang to meet them, and then with one daughter on each knee, Myrtilla playing with his long curling beard he went on :

"Perhaps your mother has told you of the circumstances connected with your loss. Probably if you had died and we had followed your remains to the sepulchre, time would have reconciled us to your loss. But the anxiety, the harassing care, the ten thousand nameless fears of ill which might betide you, kept you constantly in mind. For seven long, weary, never to be forgotten years, your situation, or what might be your situation, has been the burden which has hung around our necks like a millstone. Go where we would, for we tried travelling through every country in Europe, this anxiety for your welfare, knowing well into whose hands you had fallen, and that revenge of imaginary wrongs was the sweetest morsel to his lips, we could not rid ourselves of the fear that you were subjected to every species of torture."

"Look at this," he continued, drawing from his breast a locket attached by a ribbon to his neck. "This is a fac-simile of your mother a month before that black hearted wretch snatched you from our arms. See that smiling, lovely face. She was gazing at you, my son. I held you in my arms where her eye could rest on you. Now look at her and see what ravages grief has made."

It was indeed a sweet, fresh face, with the holy light of a mother's love beaming from every feature. Isaac gazed at it in silence, and then stooped down and kissed his mother's cheek.

Mr. Seixas gazed too; then with a sigh replaced it in his bosom, but rousing himself said:

"At last we heard of this place, I purchased it, and we moved here. In all our travels your mother was always ingenious in discovering likenesses to you in every boy about the size, she supposed our lost darling would have been. This excitement was so useless, and caused her so much suffering, that I gradually grew to hate boys; especially those, who like you, at all resembled our nation.

"I was instantly impressed with your appearance, and determined if I could avoid it, that my wife should never see you. I watched you as you went home on the night of our arrival, and it was on your account that I rudely refused Mrs Duncan's kind proffers of assistance. But I secretly watched you going and coming from school, and at your play about the grounds. Then you offered your life in defence of my little ones. How proud I was of that act! How often I said, I should have wished my son to be like this youth. You came into the house, and before I had time to prevent it, your mother saw you. I was not surprised at the result. It was exactly what I expected. Day and night she called you her boy. One convulsion followed another until I determined to leave home and try to forget. When she grew more calm, we returned after a promise on her part to make no effort to see you.

"I am almost ashamed to say how often I went to the attic to watch for you. I had already told the doctor the occasion of his patient's relapse; and he offered to make inquiries of Mrs. Duncan in reference to you. The answer left no doubt on his mind that you was her own child.

" Then came your bouquet with the name 'Isaac' on the card. How could I wonder that it threw her into the most terrible convulsions since it stirred my heart to its depths! I became envious of Mrs. Duncan for the possession of such a child, while at the same time I sought to find some excuse for hating you, for thrusting you out of sight. I had selected with great care a little testimonial of our gratitude, and while doing it was trying to harden my heart against you.

" You had a habit of gazing up at the house as you passed, little imagining how I watched and treasured up every look. You bore the impress of our lost boy in every feature. I cannot describe the contradictory emotions I experienced when you went away; joy that you would for a time be where your mother could not be annoyed by the sight of your face, and sorrow that even these slight glimpses of the past should be removed. But soon I was myself called from home. In the morning I arose free; the setting sun found me in prison, awaiting my trial for larceny. "I knew by whose means I was there; but let that pass now. My brother's power to revenge himself upon me has ceased forever. He died confessing his crimes, and among them worst of all, your abduction from home; but his strength failed before he could tell where I should find you. I raved in my cell like a madman.

"Then the doctor came and found me released; he told me the joyful news; but there were sacred duties I must fulfil before I could embrace my son. My brother had told me the names of the persons he had defrauded and also consigned to me the means to return the stolen goods, for which crime I had been arrested. All this with the efficient help of the good physician I accomplished, and then turned my face homeward. I gave my imagination wing, and could see you sitting by your mother, kneeling at her feet; and she with smiles and tears lavishing her caresses. I could see my little girls hanging about their new found brother, teasing him with a thousand questions. Then my thoughts recurred to myself. Will he love the man who has treated him so harshly? Will he forgive the seeming rudeness?"

He stopped and gazed in Isaac's eyes; and the boy, with a sudden gush of tenderness, flew into his father's arms.

"I loved you from the first, father," he said, when he grew composed. "I used to talk about you all the time. I dreamed that I was a Jew. I couldn't understand why I thought so much of you all, when you seemed to hate me.'

There was a pause full of feeling, and then the boy added in a lower tone; "Though I am a Jew, I am not like them in one thing. I believe Jesus Christ is the Messiah promised to Abraham, and I love him as my Saviour."

"You speak blasphemy, boy! but" (he checked himself as he caught a glance of anxious entreaty from his wife,) "we wont talk of that now. I am too happy and too thankful now to the God who made us all to enter into any argument. Tell me of the years that have passed since you were snatched from our arms. Had you any recollection of your earlier years to produce the feeling of interest in us?"

"I can scarcely tell. I had sometimes confused recollections of a different home; and I used often to dream of events which I now suppose, really had occurred; but as I never heard any one speak of these things I supposed they were *mere* dreams."

"Was Mrs. Duncan kind to you?"

Isaac roused at this question; the clear olive tint in his cheeks kindling into warmth and richness by the recollection of all the kindness he had received from a stranger.

"She was all that a mother can ever be," he exclaimed vehemently. "I claimed her love as my right, and now:"—

"Surely he does not repine at the change," ejaculated Mr. Seixas with a frown, as his son unable to control himself rushed from the room.

"He loved her as any affectionate boy would do," murmured the mother. "It will take a little time to turn the current of his affection."

"I love Mrs. Duncan, too," exclaimed Myrtilla, "she is a real nice lady."

"Why did you check me when he spoke of the blasphemer, cursed be he? It is best to end such apostacy at once."

"She shook her head. He is very, *very*

earnest. It is the subject on which he likes best to talk. I have no doubt she added with a smile that he hopes to convert us all from Judaism. It is a pity my father is not alive to bring him to his senses."

The father laughed scornfully. "I am not very strict in my religious observances, I confess; but the day is far distant which will find me a convert to the Nazarene. Pshaw! he is too young to know much respecting these things. They more nearly concern the Rabbies. I shall make light of them, as boyish follies, endurable from the company into which he has fallen."

"He has a strange enthusiasm about our sect, Jesse. Mrs. Duncan knowing him to be a Jew has interested him daily in them as God's chosen people, to whom were entrusted the books of the law."

"And will he dare now to abjure his nation

ality, to give up all the rights, privileges and glories of a child of Abraham?"

"No, he glories in them all. He talks by the hour of the splendor of our temple; the costliness of the sacrifices; the wisdom of our judges, and the sagacity of our prophets."

"I shall take him to the synagogue. Rabbi Ben David will speedily set him right. If he likes, he himself shall be educated for a Rabbi."

Again she shook her head. "You will see," she responded, "that it will be no easy task to change his views. These seven years have been fatal to him as well as to us."

"Then I throw all our obligation to Mrs. Duncan to the winds. If knowing him to be 'a Jew she has taught him the doctrines most abhorrent to our race, she deserves the severest punishment we can inflict, and that will be to forbid Isaac from speaking to her."

CHAPTER XI.

HOME NOT HOME.

THE entrance of the boy with marks of weeping brought the conversation to a sudden close.

Mr. Seixas rang the bell, hastily declaring he was famishing with hunger, and then wondered where the doctor could be keeping himself.

Esther who had run to her brother and was trying to coax him from his grief said:

" The doctor went away in the carriage long ago."

In half an hour the whole family including

Mrs. Seixas were sitting around the richly spread board.

Isaac accustomed from his earliest remembrance to the saying of grace bowed his head for that purpose, when his father not noticing it asked:

"My son, have you ever been to the synagogue?"

There was a short pause; and then the boy answered:

"No, sir, mamma was going to take me there when I came here."

"Do you mean Mrs. Duncan," with a slight frown.

"Yes, sir."

"Then you had better say so. Your mamma will take a piece of steak, perhaps, if you will pass her plate."

Isaac's temper was roused; and he longed to say; "I never shall call Mrs. Duncan any name but mamma;" yet with a thought of her teachings he made an effort to restrain himself. He passed the plate without a word, biting his lips to keep back the too ready tears.

Conscious that he was taking the wrong method with his high spirited boy, and not at all understanding the motives which prompted him to self control, the gentleman tried to give the conversation a mirthful turn; but nothing he could say brought a smile to the face of the sorrowing boy. He felt that he had been insulted, and what was more, that Mrs. Duncan had been insulted. He could scarcely swallow a mouthful he thought.

"Oh, why need this discovery have been made? Why was not I her son in reality?" swelled the fountain of grief till it well nigh over-flowed.

Mr. Seixas, without appearing to do so, watched him closely. After he had carved the meat, and the servant had waited on them all, he asked his wife if she would take a drive, and then turning to Isaac:

"Have you learned to ride horseback?"

"Yes, sir."

"Ah, I must get you a horse."

"I have a good one now, sir, that mamma bought me. I have a pony, too."

"Yes, the one you had when Abigail was hurt," suggested Myrtilla, eagerly.

"But they are not yours, now, Isaac."

"Why not, sir?"

"Think a moment;" he said, trying to be conciliatory, "and you will see that circumstances have changed since they were given you."

"Then I have nothing, sir," with another flash from his eye. "The clothes that I have on and everything else that I call mine, belongs to her, to my mamma."

The last word was said defiantly.

"You certainly have a watch, my boy."

"I cannot accept that, sir. I have never taken it from the box but once. I didn't want any pay for doing what I did."

The boy's eyes were so bright and the color in his cheeks and lips so brilliant, that the father could not help saying to himself:

"What a handsome fellow! I like his spirit too, though he is rather high-strung. Presently he answered with a laugh; "You'll repent of that decision; I think the watch is a handsome one."

The young Hebrew scorned to reply. He longed to get up and run away, and wake up the next morning to find himself in his dear old chamber, with his mother leaning over the couch as she often did to awake him.

The attempt at cheerfulness, or indeed, at any thing like general conversation, was a failure. Mrs. Seixas, still weak, grew nervous with fear of what would be said, and after making a very light repast, expressed a wish to return to her chamber; her husband rose instantly to carry her there, and then Isaac exclaimed with a sigh:

"How very long this day has been!"

When the gentleman returned, he saw the boy walking quickly down the avenue on the way home, as he persisted in calling Mrs. Duncan's.

"I'll put a stop to that if I am obliged to sell my place in order to do it," was his angry reflection. "It is easy to see he has not been well disciplined."

If he could have heard the conversation which passed between the lady and her dear boy during the next hour, he might have judged differently.

Rushing into the parlor, Isaac threw himself on the sofa and buried his face in his hands.

"Isaac, my son."

Mrs. Duncan spoke in a low, calm voice which usually soothed him, but comparing it with his father's ringing tones, it now roused him to greater indignation in her behalf.

"I may as well give up," he exclaimed, "I never can be good again. He forbids me to call you mamma; but I wont obey him. I owe you every thing; and I love you ten million times better than I do him. He says that I have nothing; that circumstances are changed since you gave me my horse and my clothes, and every thing else. Oh dear! I can't endure it."

"Isaac! Isaac! Stop or you will break my heart! Is this the way you take to win your friends to love the Saviour; to show them that the Master you are trying to serve, was meek and mild? You are angry, my dear child, or you would not talk to me in that tone."

Covering her face with her handkerchief she too wept. All the morning she had been striving to find comfort in the thought that in the society of his kindred, Isaac would be happy; perhaps more so than he had ever been;—that

God had, in his all-wise providence led the parents to this place, with a merciful purpose of making their son an instrument of their salvation. Retiring again and again to her closet she had entreated her Father in heaven that these happy results might follow the late discovery; that her boy might so exhibit the spirit and temper of the Lamb of God, as to bring all he held dear, not only to a formal acknowledgment of his Messiahship, but to receive him as the Saviour of their souls.

But now to see Isaac exhibiting so much anger and bitterness on this first day of his trial, when it might be supposed every one would conspire to make him happy, was indeed, a test of her faith.

Mrs. Duncan was naturally cheerful, and seldom until within a few days, had her son seen her weep. At sight of her tears for him, therefore, he threw himself on the floor at her feet, and with a low cry gave way to a passionate burst of grief.

For a while the lady made no effort to soothe him; indeed, she was unable to control her own emotions; but at length she laid her hand on his head as of old, and began to weave her fingers among his raven tresses.

His sobs grew less violent and at last he murmured:

"I am not angry now, mamma; but I am very miserable."

"Tell me all," she said, "that is in your heart."

"I was very, very angry; and when I meant to be so gentle, obedient and loving. I can never tell him about Jesus now. Can you think of no method of undoing the effect of your passion? Will you let him believe that the religion of Jesus leads to such anger?"

"But, mamma, when I spoke to him of Jesus and told him I loved him as my Saviour, I had not then been angry, and he called me a blasphemer. Why was that?"

"I will tell you some other time; the question now is with yourself. You have pierced the heart of the Friend whom you profess to love, by giving way to anger, and that toward your father. You know what God's command is: 'Let all bitterness, wrath, anger, clamour, and evil speaking, be put away from you, with all malice;' And again: 'be ye kind one to another, tender hearted, forgiving one another, even as God for Christ's sake hath forgiven you.'"

"Will he think more of this dear Friend, when he knows these lovely precepts are his, and will he think less of you when you confess that in a moment of passion you have belied them; forgetting that you are his, having been bought with a price, and acting out the evil still dwelling in you?"

For one moment the young Hebrew gazed earnestly in her eyes as if he did not exactly comprehend; but then starting to his feet the color flashed all over his face as he exclaimed:

"I know what you mean now, mamma; and I'll do it, but oh how much easier it is to be good while with you! I'll go now," he added, starting for the door. Half way down the avenue, he returned and with a quivering lip said:

"Kiss me, please, mamma. He may forbid my coming here again."

"Yes, my love; I pray for you continually that you may be guided and strengthened in the path of duty. When you are tempted to anger lift up your heart to your Saviour who is yearning over you. And remember always that I love you, and am asking God to bless you.

She kissed his cheek repeatedly, and then with dewy eyes watched him till he entered his father's door.

CHAPTER XII.

THE JEWISH CHRISTIAN BOY.

MR. and Mrs. Seixas were warmly discussing the character of their son when he entered. They were seated in her chamber, where she sat as usual in her lounging chair, and as the doors were open he overheard her say in continuation of some excuse she had made for him:

"But he is not like his sisters, yielding and gentle; he is naturally like you, impetuous. You must bear with him."

And his father answered; "If this is what he calls religion, I want none of it."

These words quickened his pulse and softened his countenance.

He went forward eagerly and seizing his father's hand said :

"I have done wrong. I was angry, and said I would not obey you. I love Mrs. Duncan so dearly ; and she has been so very kind to me, when but for her I should have died ; that for a moment, I forgot what she has often told me, that the best way to show affection for friends is to follow their teachings."

"It's noble of you to confess it, my son ; now will you tell me what teachings of her's you refer to ?"

In a minute I will ; but I want to confess something else. I have done worse, far worse."

Mrs. Seixas started forward looking extremely anxious while Isaac with a bright spot burning in either cheek, and his eyes cast down to the floor, went on :

"I told you this morning that I loved the Saviour, but I am afraid I do not ; I have forgotten his commands, too. I dishonored him. I indulged anger toward my father when he says: 'Be ye kind one to another, tender hearted forgiving one another, even as God for Christ's sake hath forgiven you.'"

"I heard what you said about my religion. It was because I forgot my religion that I did so very wrong."

Mr. Seixas was more moved than he cared to have known. Rising, he walked toward the window, but presently turned back to say:

"I am proud that I have a son who is not ashamed to acknowledge that he has done wrong. You may be sure your confession not only exalts you in my estimation; but it gives me a more favorable opinion than I was inclined to take of your friends." The last was said with a laugh; and he added in the same tone; "it isn't strange that, being constantly in the society of the Gentiles, you should imbibe their ideas to the prejudice of your character as a Jew. Some time I will take you to the synagogue, and introduce you to a learned friend of mine, a Rabbi, who will soon convince you of your error on the subject of the Nazarene.

Isaac roused at this, and was about to say :

"Nothing in the world can alter my views," when meeting an imploring glance from his mother he checked himself.

"Will you take a drive with us?" he asked presently, taking Isaac's hand in both his and pressing it warmly.

"I will accompany you on horseback," he answered, glancing toward his father.

"You have acted so well, my son, that I am willing you should ask Mrs. Duncan to allow you the use of your horse until I can procure one suitable for you."

Bouyant in spirits our young Hebrew was now almost as happy as he had been miserable a short time before, and catching his cap from the table was soon running down the avenue, all the way making earnest resolves to curb his temper for the future whatever provocation might arise.

Great was his disappointment on reaching home, to find the lady had gone out for the afternoon. He went to the stable, however, and telling John he wanted his horse saddled, he ran back to address his mamma a note, which he left on her table where it could not fail to meet her eye on her return. It was as follows:

"Dear, Precious Mamma:

I have not been forbidden to call you so in writing; but I can never, *never* cease to feel that you are my mamma whom God gave me to help me to become a good boy.

"I did confess, and my father seemed pleased with my conduct. I am going to ride now on Racer, to accompany the rest of the family who go in the phæton. Father wishes me to ask for the use of Racer till he can procure me a horse. I know I shall never love any other animal as I do my own beautiful one; but I am trying to be pleased and to seek for peace. Will you please stand by your chamber window at sunset? Perhaps I may not be able to see you unless you do. I love you, dear, dear mamma, more than I can find words to tell you. It was you who put the good thought into my mind. I am glad now I acted upon it.

Your own loving son,
Isaac."

The ride was a very pleasant one. Isaac as having a superior knowledge of the country, chose the direction they were to take, riding close to the carriage and conversing with his sisters in a merry tone.

"See how well he rides," exclaimed Mrs. Seixas in answer to her husband.

"Yes, he is a thoroughly trained equestrian. He looks every whit a Jew. I must introduce him to my friends."

"Let us take time to get well acquainted with him first, was the earnest suggestion.

Myrtilla and Esther were continually calling after their brother, if he for a moment gave the rein to his horse to exhibit his skill as a horseman, telling him he would be lost if he went by himself; or that they might need him if any wild animals came in the way. It was a new pleasure to be accompanied by their brother, and gave great additional interest to the drive.

When they reached home our young friend saw by his mamma's curtain being still down that she had not returned, and therefore, gave his horse to John without going into the house and went directly to his mother's room.

She held out a note with a smile saying: "Did you know of this?"

He took it from her and read with quickened pulse:

"Mr. Seixas:

The horse Racer was given to your son as a reward for controlling his temper perfectly for one month. If you do not consider it a suitable animal for him, you can sell it or dispose of it in any way you please. The creature is his; and I assure you was recommended to me as thoroughly sound and well-trained for the saddle. Will you have the goodness to tell Isaac that I have been suddenly called away from home for a few days to visit my friend in Saratoga who is very ill?

With Respect, Yours,

Emma Duncan."

"A very lady-like epistle," remarked Mr.

Seixas, coming in from the garden and perusing it. Racer is yours then, won by self control. I congratulate you, my boy; really, this Mrs. Duncan improves on acquaintance."

"I wish you only knew how good she is," said the boy, with an impulsive gesture. "I used to be awfully passionate when I was young."

The gentleman smiled. "You are not very aged yet, but speaking of temper I am afraid it is a family trait, your uncle and I used to be called, 'those passionate Jews.'"

"Shall I continue to attend school, father? I am getting behind my class."

"I should prefer sending you to a better school in the city of New York; but as your mother cannot give her consent to your leaving home at present, you had better go on with your studies here. Come with me to the library; I should like to hear how far you are advanced in your education."

The next hour was passed to the mutual delight of father and son. Mr. Seixas learned that Isaac had a clear knowledge of the primary branches; could read and spell accurately, and had a fair knowledge of geography, grammar and arithmetic. Beside this he had gone through the Latin grammar and was beginning to translate.

The boy learned that his father had a liberal education, was a fine classical scholar; could communicate his ideas clearly, and was patient in teaching, and would therefore, be a great aid to him in his studies.

Bed-time came, and the young Hebrew retired to his room more happy and more at peace with himself than he had ever supposed he could be in his father's house, or any where away from his loved mamma.

"I can pray for them now," he said to himself, "and hope my prayer will be answered, for I have tried to please my Saviour."

The next morning, which was Wednesday, he returned to his lessons; and until Saturday, was doubly busy in making up the recitations he had lost. One hour, too, of every afternoon was required by the teacher in preparation of an advance lesson, and this was spent in the library, where his father had given him a window with a desk for his books. There he soon learned that with his father's ever ready assistance, he could advance far more rapidly than he had done, and formed a sudden resolution to overtake the class above him, and go on with those older boys who had always excited his admiration by the critical manner in which their recitations were prepared.

Saturday, the Jewish Sabbath, was a holiday, and Isaac, unmindful of its being considered holy time was running down stairs to meet his sisters who had been impatiently calling him, when Abigail said, softly:

"Would Mrs. Duncan approve your going to the synagogue?"

"Yes, indeed, she promised to take me there."

"Your father will take you and your sisters to-day. Your mother has bid me get them dressed in season. It is not like your manner of worship though."

Abigail had been twice to the church in the village, unknown to her master and mistress, and was now greatly concerned as to her duty in regard to acknowledging publicly the change in her views. She had intended to consult Mrs. Duncan, but as the lady was away, she resolved to watch the turn of events with the son.

Isaac frankly expressed his pleasure at the thought of accompanying his father to the synagogue, which was only four miles distant, though he grew a little pale when told that they should meet Rabbi Ben David, who would probably return with them and pass the night.

CHAPTER XIII.

THE SYNAGOGUE AND RABBI.

DURING the ride the young Hebrew learned from his father that the synagogues were first used after the Babylonish captivity; and then only for purposes of instruction; but that after the destruction of the temple by the Romans, religious services were performed in them.

"Do they have a sermon preached there?" he inquired.

"No, not a sermon according to the Gentile method; the liturgy is read and prayers offered, and sometimes instruction is given. The prayers you will find are repeated aloud by the whole assembly."

"And have they no choir, no organ, nor singing," was the surprised inquiry?

The gentleman laughed aloud; while Myrtilla said:

"Oh such funny chanting, little boys too!"

On entering the porch, Isaac saw with astonishment that his father committed the twins to the care of a woman who took them up to the gallery while he motioned him to follow into the body of the house.

Presently taking off his cap, therefore, he stepped softly toward the green baize door which separated the porch from the main room, feeling as if the place was holy ground, his breath coming so quickly that he did not notice those about him until seated in a prominent slip by his father.

It was just time for the service to commence. Mr. Seixas motioned for his son to put on his cap; and he then noticed with great surprise that all the males present wore hats. He watched the proceedings with great curiosity, as his father in common with the rest arose, and taking from a corner of the pew where it was folded the fringed garment worn during service, threw it over his shoulders; then with his prayer book in his hand, he began to repeat aloud in unison with the whole assembly the opening prayer for the day.

This was recited with such rapidity, and as the listener thought, with so little emotion, that it sounded to him like a mere sing-song, of which, as it was in Hebrew he could not of course understand one word.

This was followed in rapid succession by the reading of the law, also in Hebrew, by a man standing in the large enclosure in the centre of the house, and who Mr. Seixas informed his son was Rabbi Ben David.

He was a man of ordinary height, with

spectacles, and a cap with a tassel, on his head. His vesture or mantle was elaborately ornamented with fringes. He held his head close to the parchment or scroll containing the sacred words of the law and rattled off the words as if his chief object in life was to finish the task.

Directly in front of Isaac and within plain sight of the Rabbies and readers in the desk, were two boys playing at marbles; while in other slips were men who evidently heard little, and cared less for the service; but who, the boy shrewdly suspected, were making a bargain. To be sure they joined loudly in the Hebrew "amens," but instantly resumed their whisperings.

When the reading was finished, and the sacred scrolls reverently rolled up, restored to their gilded cases, and carried on the shoulders of the men appointed to the service, to the holy place, before which the curtain was drawn, there was more interest. The men all rose; and Isaac could see that the women in the gallery opposite did also, and turning their faces toward the holy of holies, joined in the closing prayer.

The breaking up was very sudden; and then every one seemed to be at liberty to do what he pleased.

Hastily rolling up his fringed vesture and tossing it into the corner of the slip, Mr. Seixas went to the desk and spoke some earnest words to the Rabbi.

Isaac could not doubt they referred to him, as they constantly looked in that direction; Ben David continually raising his hands and eyes to heaven, as if in astonishment.

"And this is he! truly a goodly Israelite," said the Rabbi, at last approaching. Then laying his hand on the boy's head, he said with real feeling:

"The God of his father Abraham, the

Angel that delivered Jacob from all evil, bless the lad."

"You must come with us and help us give praise for the mercy which has restored a son as it were from the dead," urged Mr. Seixas.

"That I will with pleasure," and after sending a message to his family, they walked out together to the carriage, the boy being conscious of many anxious looks directed at him.

In the town where the synagogue was situated were many friends of Mrs. Duncan; and Isaac had often visited them with her; but these Jews were all strangers. He sighed as he cast a lingering glance behind him, for he had no desire to come again; he also sighed as he remembered Mrs. Duncan's words: "There is no vitality there." Their prayers are a usless form of words, because not offered in the only name which can gain them acceptance with the Father; the name of Jesus Christ the Lord.

They were scarcely seated in the phaeton before Mr. Seixas, who felt that it was desirable to improve the time when his wife was not present, began by saying:

"My boy, though a thorough Jew in looks, and I believe in pride of his ancestors, has acquired with his Gentile education the belief in the Impostor, as the Messiah promised to Israel. I look to you to help me convince him from our sacred books that this man Jesus cannot be he."

Isaac, who was seated directly in front of Ben David saw his countenance change. He turned quickly toward the hills, looming in the distance as if only intent on the prospect, but in reality to send up a secret petition to him who knows the hearts of all, to give him wisdom and strength to endure calmly whatever should be said to him.

"Is this your first attendance at the synagogue?" inquired Ben David in a kindly tone.

"Yes, sir."

"And how were you pleased?"

This was a difficult question to answer as it would not do to tell why he did not like it. He therefore replied evasively:

"It was very strange to me; and much of it I could not understand. I liked to see the fringed garments which I have read about in my Bible. I liked the sound of the Hebrew in the reading. I wondered while you were chanting whether it was in the same kind of a pulpit that Jesus read and talked to the people."

At the blessed name of Jesus the Rabbi's face grew dark.

"The vile Impostor," he murmured; "Cursed be the day when he was born."

Mr. Seixas's glance was fastened on his son's

face, and he actually started to see the lad's eyes flash with horror.

"I wont hear you speak so of my Saviour," he exclaimed; "You don't know him — what he has done — how he came from heaven and gave his life for us — for Jews first, and for Gentiles too. It is awfully wicked to speak of the Lord Jesus Christ, the Messiah God promised our fathers, as an Impostor. If he had never come to this world you would now have been without any hope of heaven. For he is the only way; there is no other name given among men by which any one can be saved."

"Little serpent!" hissed Ben David. Instead of a blessing to your father, you will be his curse. You are not worthy to belong to the family of the faithful."

"Hush! hush!! Ben David, this is not the way to convince him of his error," exclaimed Mr. Seixas, fearing the worst effect from this passion, while Myrtilla, catching her brother's hand, tried to pacify him by saying, softly:

"Don't mind him, Isaac; he's so cross. I love Jesus; he's so kind to little children."

These words, though pronounced in a whisper, were audible to all; and so enraged the Rabbi, that he lost all control of himself. He launched upon the head of the pale youth a perfect torrent of abuse, ending at last by saying, it would be a blessing to all connected with him to find him dead in his bed the next morning, rather than to have him live to spread abroad his horrible blasphemies.

It was all in vain that Mr. Seixas tried to stop him; or that the children burst into loud cries of alarm. Speak he would, especially as from the increasing pallor of Isaac's face, he thought he had intimidated him.

Little did he imagine that the prayer for strength to endure had been answered, and that every word he said only confirmed the boy's love in the precepts of his Divine Friend.

A passage which was found in his morning reading occurred to him: "By their fruits ye shall know them." While his father with considerable severity was taking his friend to task for his harshness, he was saying to himself: "If such are the fruits of rejecting the Saviour, I hope I may cling to his cross more firmly than ever."

From his own experience with his son, Mr. Seixas expected to hear him retort in the same strain; how much, then, was he surprised when the lad said, meekly:

"I pity you, sir. I pity every body who has no Saviour. I am often angry myself, and say harsh words; but what would become of me if I could not confess my sins to my Heavenly Father and ask him to forgive them?"

"Do you suppose, Isaac, that we never go

to God and confess our sins?" asked his father.

"I know you say prayers; but they cannot be accepted."

"Vile deceiver! How dare you say that," retorted Ben David, fiercely.

"I do not say it; God says it. He spoke in a voice from heaven, saying: "This is my beloved son in whom I am well pleased;" and in another place he says: "If any man tries to get into heaven any other way but by Christ he is a thief and a robber; that no one can be saved except for his sake."

"Did not God appoint offerings and sacrifices to take away sin?" inquired his father, seeing that the Rabbi was in no frame for an argument.

"Yes, sir; he commanded lambs to be offered; but they were only types of Jesus Christ, the Lamb of God, who was to take away the sins of the world. There are no sacrifices offered now; and no scape-goat to bear the sins of all the people into the wilderness, so what should we do without?"

"Cease to speak the name of the blasphemer, and I will tell you," said the Rabbi, drawing from his breast pocket a prayer book. Turning to a page near the commencement, he read:

"Sovereign of the Universe! It is clearly known unto thee, that whilst the holy temple was established, if a man sinned he brought an offering, of which they only offered its fat and its blood; yet didst thou in thine abundant mercy grant him pardon; but now because of our iniquities, the holy temple is destroyed; and we have neither sanctuary nor priest to atone for us. O may it, therefore, be acceptable in thy presence, that the diminution of my fat and blood, which hath been diminished this day, may be accounted as fat offered and placed on the altar, and thus be accepted of me!*"

Isaac glanced at the round face and stocky figure of the Rabbi, and could not restrain a smile as he thought; "very little of your fat and blood has been diminished this day." But seeing his father look displeased at his mirth, he drew from his breast pocket a small Bible, and turning to Micah read a portion his mamma had pointed out to him, while they were studying on this subject.

"Here is what Micah, our own prophet tells us," he said solemnly, as Ben David shut his book triumphantly, and restored it to its place.

"Will the Lord be pleased with thousands of rams, or with ten thousands of rivers of oil? Shall I give my first-born for my transgressions, the fruit of my body for the sin of my soul? *** What doth the Lord require of

P. 37 Jewish Prayer Book.

thee, but to do justly, to love mercy, and to walk humbly with thy God?"

"I don't see how that applies, Isaac. The Rabbies and all good Jews try to live up to those rules, and you acknowledge that is all which is required."

"But you see, father, Micah has just been speaking of the coming of Christ; he says: "But thou Bethlehem Ephratah, though thou be little among the thousands of Judah, yet out of thee shall he come forth unto me that is to be ruler in Israel; whose goings forth have been from old, from everlasting."

At this moment the carriage dashed up to the steps of their own door, greatly to the relief of Ben David, if one might judge by the alacrity with which he prepared to alight.

CHAPTER XIV.

FROM SYNAGOGUE TO CHURCH.

THE dinner to which Mr. Seixas invited Ben David was a luxurious one, though in accordance with Jewish law, every article had been prepared the previous day. It was soon evident to Isaac that there was no danger of his being remembered until the duty of discussing the delicate viands had been properly disposed of. As one course followed another, he had opportunity to reflect upon the events of the morning. Compared with this man, his father had been calm and even kind, though he acknowledged to himself little had passed to make him hopeful; yet he could not repress a feeling that if his parents would listen calmly to Mrs. Duncan's arguments in favor of Christ, they would be convinced he was the Messiah long expected by the Jews.

After dinner, he easily gained his mother's permission to take his sisters out for a walk, so that only at the supper-table did he have an opportunity of seeing the Rabbi again.

Rising the next morning at the usual hour, he found no preparations for the morning meal. Being anxious to be in season for the Sabbath school, he inquired of Abigail how soon it would be ready.

"At ten," she answered curtly. "So you had better eat yours, and go to church if you wish, before your father leaves his room."

"Why?" he asked in surprise.

"Do you suppose he will let you go to church to be strengthened in your love of the Saviour? she retorted bitterly. Ben David, bigoted old Rabbi as he is, will uphold him in any severity, which will bring you to renounce Jesus."

"They may cut off my hands, and my feet, and my head too; but they can't make me do that," exclaimed the boy, rising and walking the room; "but Abigail, I had no idea father would refuse me the privilege of going to church, and to Sabbath school."

"What do you go there for?"

"To learn of Jesus," reciting the line of a favorite hymn.

"Tell him that, and see what he will say," she repeated with a bitter smile.

Isaac threw himself into a chair and hid his face in his hands.

Abigail went to and fro, often casting a glance at him, wondering what he could do, but little dreaming of the struggle going on in his breast.

"What shall I do? What is duty?" was the ever recurring question. "Go to church and

Sabbath school, or try to please my father by staying at home?"

The little French clock striking eight aroused him at last, and without a word to any one he went back to his chamber. This was adjoining his sisters, and he heard them chatting together in suppressed voices.

"Come in here," he said, opening his door; "come and we will have a Sabbath school."

The next hour flew by so quickly that he was surprised when he heard the little silver bells chiming nine, and at the same time the servant sounding the rising bell. In one quarter of an hour he must start for Sunday school if he went at all. Leaving his sisters with Abigail he crossed the hall and knocked at his father's door.

"May I speak with you a minute, sir?"

"Are you dressed already?" asked his mother.

"Yes, ma'am; and should have eaten my

breakfast and been off to the Sunday school, but "—

" But what?" asked his father sternly.

" Abigail told me you would not be pleased; I will tell the whole truth. I tried to convince myself that as you had never forbidden me to go, I might do so; but the fifth command is, 'honor thy father and thy mother.' and I knew it would not be honoring you to do what perhaps you would not approve."

Mrs. Seixas's eyes expressed her appreciation of his conduct. The gentleman had turned abruptly to his wash bowl, and the boy could not judge of his feelings.

Finding they did not speak he added, earnestly:

" I should be very glad to go if you will allow me, father?"

" I'm sure husband it can't hurt him if he learns to be so obedient and truthful there. I wish the little girls might go too."

"Oh, mother, that would make me so very happy!"

He kneeled by the bed, and pressed his lips to her cheek, his face lighted with enthusiasm.

"I have been telling your mother, my son," began Mr. Seixas in a subdued tone, "that considering the circumstances, you conducted yourself well toward Rabbi Ben David, who did not pursue the course I should have wished. As a reward for that and for your frankness this morning, I give you leave to spend the day as you please."

"Thank you, dear father, I will try, indeed I will, to be a dutiful son to you, and not to prove the curse that Ben David predicts."

"Pshaw! he was in a passion when he said that. Go and forget."

"And ask Abigail to give the children their breakfast that they may go with you," added his mother.

"I never saw him look so handsome,"

remarked his father when he had left the room.

"Strong as a lion in defence of what he considers truth; and yet gentle as a lamb with his sisters."

"I have learned a lesson this morning, Sophia. If I wish to govern Isaac at all, I must govern him through his affections. He has a loving heart."

"Like yours, Jesse."

"He argued well too, astonishingly well for a boy of his years. He seemed much more at home with the Scriptures than Ben David did. I never saw my friend appear so badly."

"What if his friend Jesus should prove the true Messiah predicted by our prophets?"

The lady said this timidly as if fearful of the result of her expressing even a doubt. To her surprise her husband answered, by asking:

"What would your father say to such a question from your lips?"

"He went on with his toilet, but after a few

moments added: "Isaac put some tough questions to the Rabbi. I thought of them in the night. You know I have never troubled myself about doctrines, leaving that to the priests; but it is true, as the boy says, that a scapegoat was sent once a year to the wilderness, bearing off the sins of the people; now it is a long time since our temple, and consequently our worship, was destroyed. From that time we have had no offerings for sin. If Ben David were disposed, I have no doubt he could explain how it is, that we approach God; but:"—

"What did he say to Isaac?" was the eager inquiry.

"Very little; he only quoted from our prayer book, and really, Sophia, the prayer seemed to me too absurd to find credence among men of sense, as the Jews undoubtedly are."

"What do Christians say about it?"

"They say, Christ is the great sacrifice to which all others pointed. Now if I can learn that it was just at the hour of his advent all our offerings ceased, that will be one strong point of his Messiahship fully established."

Directly after breakfast Ben David expressed a wish to return home; and his host at once rang the bell and ordered the carriage to be made ready to take him there. Nothing more was said of Isaac until he was just about to leave when Mr. Sexias remarked:

"There is one question I wish to ask you. Our Scripture says: 'The sceptre shall not depart from Judah nor a lawgiver from between his feet till Shiloh come.' Now it is a sad fact that the sceptre has departed from Judah and the legislative power has long ago passed from his offspring, or between his feet, into the hands of the Gentiles. What must we infer from this fact?"

"Infer any thing you please," was the fierce retort. "I have been deceived in you. I denounce you as a follower of the Nazarene," shouted the Rabbi, almost beside himself with rage. "I spit upon him. Cursed be ye all!"

"You will regret this when your passion has had time to cool," answered Mr. Seixas calmly. "If I had a doubt before, it is confirmed by you. If our Rabbies cannot or will not teach the people the doctrines, how can they expect us to remain true to the religion of our father Abraham?"

He then went to the door and ordered the servant to drive rapidly, as he wished Mrs. Seixas to take the air before the heat of the day, and Ben David took his departure without a word or look of farewell.

In the evening, Mr. Seixas was passing the door of the nursery, when he heard a low sound which attracted his attention.

Lingering for a moment he distinguished the voice of Isaac, and the twins repeating a form of prayer which, as he stood there, he acknowledged to be one of the most beautiful he had ever heard. Myrtilla and Esther joined in it readily, as if it were familiar, and then Isaac added a few brief petitions of his own, asking: "the God of Abraham to be their God as he was the God of their fathers, and to make them a happy family, united in the best of bonds, love to the dear Saviour who had shed his blood to save their souls."

He opened the door as the voice ceased, and saw the twins with their arms around their brother's neck, kissing him good night, while Abigail stood at the farther end of the room waiting for them.

"Come to the library, my son," said Mr. Seixas, in a serious tone.

The lad obeyed, fearing he had displeased his father by teaching his sisters the Christian's prayer.

"I must remember his kindness this morning," he said to himself. He had learned a lesson, too.

"Sit down, my son," said the gentleman with a smile: "I heard the form of prayer you have taught your sisters; and I must confess that it is beautiful in its briefness, comprehending both our desires concerning God and our temporal good."

"Where did you find it?"

"It is the prayer taught by Christ to his disciples. We call it the Lord's prayer," replied Isaac, his eyes kindling with pleasure.

A flush of surprise appeared for a moment on the gentleman's countenance as he exclaimed:

"Ah! I was not aware of that; but he instantly recovered himself, and added; then it is in the New Testament as Christians call the addition, they have made to the Bible, I suppose?"

Isaac's color mounted to his temples, but

one thought of Ben David calmed him, and he answered with a smile; "Yes, sir."

There was a pause. Mr. Seixas was evidently at a loss how to proceed, and then he said: "You know I do not believe that our Messiah, our Deliverer has come; but I disapprove of the method taken by Ben David to convince you of your error. I wish to argue the case frankly with you, and convince you from the law and the prophets that this Nazarene you call Jesus, cannot be Judah's Lion prophesied of by our fathers."

"I would like it, dear father, except for one reason; you are a great scholar while I am an ignorant boy. I feel sure that I am right; and that Jesus is he who was sent for the deliverance of our people; but I may not be able to explain every thing that our Bible tells us about it. I wish you would let me ask Mrs. Duncan, to come over and talk with you?"

The father frowned. "Mrs Duncan though kind to you is a Gentile. I have nothing to do with her belief. It is for your good, I wish to talk upon this subject. This was the truth, but not the *whole* truth. Scarcely a moment of the day had the subject been absent from his mind, and unconsciously to himself the words and still more the actions of his son had led him to the inquiry; "What is truth?"

"I am ready to answer your questions, father, though I am sorry now I did not pay better attention to what my mamma, — (Mrs. Duncan I mean,) — I do try to remember what you told me, sir; — taught me. I did not know then, why she talked so much of the Israelites, whom she always called God's chosen people; nor why she explained so carefully from the Old Testament, the prophecies relating to him, which are so exactly fulfilled in the New."

"You were talking of Micah's prophecy in the carriage; how does that apply to Jesus Christ? May I be forgiven, if I sin in speaking the name!"

"I was telling him that Micah said; out of Bethlehem should come one who should be Ruler or King in Israel, and here in the second chapter of Matthew reference is made to the same prophecy, after recording the birth of Christ. 'And thou Bethlehem in the land of Juda art not the least among the princess of Juda, for out of thee shall come a Governor that shall rule my people Israel.'"

"I know well, my son, that it was the design of the writer of the New Testament to make these prophecies appear to fulfil the predictions of God's holy prophets."

"There are a great many writers, sir. Most of them were ignorant men, fishermen; but God told them what to write; and there were men and women then living, who could have exposed them if they had not told the truth."

"That may be so. I have never felt much interest in these subjects; not as much perhaps as I ought to have felt. I considered them as belonging to the Rabbies."

"But we have all sinned, father;" and we all wish to be saved; if you don't believe in Jesus Christ, why don't you still offer a lamb for a burnt sacrifice?"

"All such ceremonies were abolished, my son, in the year seventy, when the temple was destroyed by the Romans under Titus. I think that in some parts of the world, altars have been built at different periods; and a few have offered sacrifices upon them; but these cases are rare.

"There is no need of them now," Isaac added eagerly. "The great sacrifice has been offered; the Lamb of God slain. May I read you our account of it?"

"Certainly, I am ready to hear any thing in the way of argument."

"Well, you know there were a great many Jews who would not receive Christ; but when they saw his miracles they believed. At last when men, women and children followed him, listening to his words, the people said he was perverting the nation, and demanded that he should be crucified. Here it is in Luke. There are three other accounts of it; but Mrs. Duncan says this is the most minute, though they all correspond." He commenced at the twenty-second chapter and read through the Gospel, without one word of comment from his father. By this time it had become so dark that he could scarcely see, and Mr. Seixas took advantage of it to end the interview.

CHAPTER XV.

A NAIL IN A SURE PLACE.

ABOUT this time the post man brought a letter, which though written two years before, caused no little excitement in the family. It was dated Nice, France, and purported to be from the nurse who had disappeared at the time Isaac had been stolen by his uncle. The writing had evidently been wet, and some parts of the letter were ·wholly unintelligible. But the legible part read as follows:

" RESPECTED MISTRESS :

This is the first opportunity I have had to send you word of your lost darling. I cannot write, which I have never regretted so much as since we were deceived by Mr. Justin Seixas; and persuaded to go with him on board a vessel bound for Havre. Isaac was well during the voyage, and soon grew reconciled to be absent from you, though at first he called for papa and mamma, pretty mamma, continually. I went with him to a convent for a few months, and then he was taken to live with a lady and gentleman who wished to adopt him. I was married soon after to one of my own countryman, servant to a great family residing here, and I have not seen your boy since. The lady seemed very fond of Isaac, and I think they will take good care of him.

Your obedient servant,
Margaret Doyle."

Mr. Seixas flew to his wife's chamber with the open letter, and asked her what she could make of it. She could make nothing of it, but suggested that Mrs. Duncan who had just returned from Saratoga, be sent for to repeat her statement of Isaac's history.

She came at once.

"Were you ever in Nice? Did you tak our boy from a convent there?" were Mr Seixas's eager inquiries.

She shook her head; and then repeated the story she had told the doctor.

"It was in New Orleans. My husband never entertained a doubt that the gentleman who brought the boy was the one who had saved his life. He urged that the mother was dead; that he was obliged to leave the country immediately; that he probably never should return; and that he would never claim the child from us."

"And yet on his dying bed he told me that the boy was in a small village in France, pretending that he could not remember the name."

"What is the date of the letter?"

"February twelfth, nearly two and a half years ago."

"And where was your brother at that time?"

"Probably in Europe."

"No doubt, then, it was written at his suggestion; perhaps by his own hand."

"What possible motive could he have had?" questioned Mrs. Seixas, indignantly.

"The same motive which prompted him to steal our heart's treasure, revenge," answered Mr. Seixas bitterly. "Yes, that is it. It is clear to me as noon-day. Even when he knew he had not five minutes to live, he perjured himself in order to send me on a fruitless voyage to France, where but for your kindness, madam, I might have spent years in search of my son."

"I suppose you have not the least doubt that Isaac is your child?"

"Doubt! no, indeed," exclaimed the mother. "Not a shadow of doubt."

"The resemblance between us is proof sufficient to satisfy any court of justice in the land," added the father.

"I suppose it must be so," murmured the lady.

"Shall you tell Isaac, husband?"

"No; it will only unsettle his mind. The letter was intended to reach us when it was supposed that we were becoming reconciled to our loss, and by inspiring hope of his recovery to arouse in our minds all the first pangs of sorrow at the terrible bereavement. It was a fiendish plot, too much in accordance with Justin's life in later years, to be much wondered at."

"Isaac, did you ever go to sea?" asked his father at dinner.

"No, sir."

"Try to remember, whether you weren't

once in a ship, with a nurse to take care of you."

The young Hebrew opened wide his eyes, the color deepening on his cheeks, as he gazed in his father's excited face.

"I can remember nothing of the kind, sir."

"And did you never have a dream of being on the water out of sight of land?"

"No, sir. Why do you ask?"

"Don't be alarmed," explained his mother, "your father has a way of trying to puzzle people."

Isaac laughed, and went on with his dinner. He was becoming better acquainted with his father every day; and every day was more in hope of his conversion.

The letter so carefully re-read and laid away, was the cause of great joy to Isaac in one particular. It drew Mrs. Duncan into the family on the terms of an intimate friend. Gradually, too, she was called into the discussions which were of almost daily occurrence between the boy and his father; and encouraged the former to pray earnestly that the hearts of the whole family might be turned to him who had been sent for the deliverance of their people.

Though neither Mrs. Duncan nor Isaac suspected it, the gentleman spent much of his time in searching the Scriptures for arguments to prove that Jesus could not be the long expected Messiah. Then he would turn to the New Testament, a copy of which Isaac had left on the little table allotted to his use, and here he confessed to himself that this same Jesus was a remarkable man; possessed of such love, meekness and wisdom, as would eminently fit him for the office of a Ruler in Israel.

One morning they were all sitting in Mrs. Seixas's chamber, when Mrs. Duncan said; "there is one prophecy with regard to the Jews which in connection with the Saviour has been so exactly fulfilled that I have often wondered it was not alluded to by your own people. This regards the dispersion of them into all lands in consequence of their rejection of the Messiah, God had sent."

"Yes," answered the gentleman with a sigh.

"Formerly I thought little upon these subjects; but the sudden death of my brother, and the goodness of the Lord in restoring my son to me, has led me to read much in our Scriptures. The glory and beauty of Israel was great; her men were mighty warriors; her women fair and lovely as the morning; but her glorious temple is destroyed; her altars in ruins; her people scattered."

"Isaac opened his Bible to the book of Deuteronomy and read: "And the Lord shall scatter thee among all people from one end of the earth even unto the other." "Here is another prophecy in Hosea," he added, turning the leaves rapidly: "My God will cast them away, because they will not hearken unto him; and they shall be wanderers among the nations."

"But the promises of the restoration of the Jews are full and very precious," rejoined Mrs. Duncan earnestly. "Do not you look for this?"

"I suppose that every Jew has some indistinct idea of God's promise to restore to us the land of our father's; but to confess the truth I have attached little importance to the subject."

"Isaac, then, though ignorant that he was a partaker in these great privileges, is unlike you in that respect. I have seen his eyes, kindle with anticipation of their coming glories. I am myself a firm believer in the restoration of God's chosen Israel not only to Divine favor, but many of them, to their own land."

"Yes, father, and when we read of all the commotion there, we used to rejoice, and say:

' God is preparing the way for his people to return.' Moses and the prophets distinctly point to the restoration not only of Judah and Benjamin, but of the long lost Ten Tribes again to inhabit the land which God gave to Abraham."

" You will remember," remarked Mrs. Duncan; "that in the service of the synagogue there is scarcely a prayer which does not plead the promise of God to bring you back?" But hear what the Lord says :

" If my covenant be not with you day and night, and if I have not appointed the ordinances of heaven and earth; then will I cast away the seed of Jacob and David my servants, so that I will not take any of his seed to be rulers over the seed of Abraham, Isaac and Jacob; for I will cause their captivity to return and have mercy on them."

" And when will these bright days dawn on our poor, down-trodden race?"

"I will read what God has said by his holy prophet Hosea: 'For the children of Israel shall abide many days without a king, and without a prince, and without a sacrifice, and without an image, and without an ephod, and without teraphim.'"

"Ah, that is all very true, too true!"

"Yes, but listen to the verse which follows: 'Afterwards shall the children of Israel return, and seek the Lord their God, and David their king; and shall fear the Lord and his goodness in the latter days.'"

"They shall obey, submit themselves to the Messiah the son of David their king. They shall look with faith on his atoning sacrifice; on this Messiah or David as he is often called; or as Zachariah says: 'they shall look on him whom they have pierced and mourn.' Jesus, when hanging on the cross was pierced by the Jews, and many looking on at the time went away mourning and weeping.

"Jeremiah, too, after speaking of the yoke long borne by his chosen Israel says: 'I will break this yoke from off thy neck, and will burst thy bonds. * * But they shall serve the Lord their God and David their king." What do you understand by this prediction? I mean as referring to you now."

"I cannot say. We have no nation,—no king."

"David you know had long been dead, and none of his descendants ever reigned over the Jews after the Babylonish captivity. Must it not refer to the kingdom of Messiah or David's son?"

"Of course, it must."

"And was not Jesus of David's line? He did not hesitate to apply to himself all the predictions of the prophets. He called himself, 'the Son of God,' 'the King of Israel,' 'the I Am,' the Pre-existant,' 'the Judge of the world.'"

"Oh father! dear father," implored Isaac, seizing and pressing his hand; why will not you acknowledge that Jesus Christ is the Messiah?"

Mr. Seixas was greatly moved, and he did not attempt to conceal it; but his countenance wore a still graver aspect when the lady said earnestly: "You may indeed acknowledge that in him all the prophecies have been fulfilled; not one jot or tittle of them have failed; and yet your soul may be in as great danger as it now is."

"I do not understand you, madam. How can that be?"

Because, though he is the Saviour promised, yet he may not be *your* Saviour. You must accept the sacrifice he has made, and thus make it yours. There were daily sacrifices at the temple; but unless each man carried his own sin-offering, his guilt was not atoned for. Christ has indeed done his part but it will be all the same to you, as if the Messiah had not yet appeared unless you have faith in him, as your Mediator, your High Priest. God is just, and cannot accept you nor forgive your sins, only through the righteousness of our Lord Jesus Christ, imputed to you and received by faith alone."

"Jeremiah says of the Jews in the latter days, not that they shall own him whom they have heretofore rejected; but 'they shall *serve* the Lord their God and David their king, whom I will raise up unto them.'"

CHAPTER XVI.

FIRST WORKS.

ON Sabbath evening Mrs. Duncan stood at the window watching the thickening clouds and wondering whether she had better go to the evening service, when she saw Mr. Seixas leave his own door and soon after walk slowly up her avenue.

There were signs of deep feeling on his countenance; and she lifted her heart in earnest prayer that he might find peace where alone it can be found, at the foot of the cross.

"I hope I do not intrude," he said, with a weary smile, as the servant opened the door of the parlor; "but indeed, what you said to me the other day has given me so many subjects for thought, I may say anxiety, that I have scarcely slept since."

While he was speaking, Mrs. Duncan felt that it would be a holy and blessed privilege to lead this child of Abraham to his Saviour; therefore, she said cordially as she extended her hand:

"You are welcome, sir, thrice welcome, when you come to talk upon such themes!"

He took the seat she pulled toward him. but seemed at a loss for words; at last she said:

"This you know is our Sabbath, changed from the seventh to the first day of the week after the ascension of our crucified Redeemer."

"Yes, I know you observe this; but I have searched in vain for any reasons why it should be so; but that is not my greatest anxiety now."

He bowed his head, — that child of Abraham, and the lady saw that his chin quivered with suppressed emotion.

It was a full minute before he spoke again, and then he said: "I am beginning to feel that I have broken the law of God. I have read over the commands God gave to our great lawgiver; and there is not one which I have not violated either in spirit or letter. I have examined our ceremonial law, too, and there are a great many offences and omissions of which I have been guilty, which were to be punished with death. I would take the fattest of bullocks, goats and rams, and slay them if I thought they would atone for my sins; but our altars are desolate and forsaken; there is no priest to go for me into the Holy of Holies and intercede in my behalf. Ever since I saw my brother die, I have felt as I never did before, the reality of death, and the necessity of preparing some sacrifice which I may take in my hand when I am summoned into the presence of my great King."

He stopped, and in the deepening twilight his companion could see that his breast heaved convulsively. Lifting up her heart in a silent petition for wisdom she said: "I know of but one sacrifice that will avail you at the court of heaven; and that is the red hand of Jesus, — the hand pierced with nails — blood-stained, but precious above all price."

"But, madam, you do not understand me. I am convinced that he is the Lord, one with the Father, King, Strength, Creator, Redeemer, and Sanctifier, whom we so often address in our liturgy, (may the Lord pardon my long unbelief;) but will he receive me? — will he allow me to share in this great atonement when I have so long rejected him, spit upon him, treated him as a vile blasphemer?

"Mr. Seixas, are you a son of Abraham? And dare you ask whether his word is true who is from everlasting and changeth not? He says: 'Come unto me, all ye, that are weary and heavy laden, and I will give you rest.' Are not you weary with bearing your sins so many years? Come and lay your burden down at the foot of his cross. I who am not a Jew, but through this goodly people have received not only the sacred books of the law, but the Prince whom I worship, beg you, one of the seed of Abraham, his chosen, to come and taste the salvation he offers you. He has shed his blood for you; died that you might live; will you not accept of life on his terms?"

"I do accept of him; alas! I have no other hope; but what am I, that he should think of me!"

She turned quickly to the thirty-third of Ezekiel, and recited rather than read the words:

" Therefore, O thou son of man, speak unto

the house of Israel; thus ye speak saying: If our transgressions and our sins be upon us and we pine away in them, how should we live? Say unto them as I live, saith the Lord God, I have no pleasure in the death of the wicked; but that the wicked turn from his way and live; turn ye, turn ye from your evil ways; for why will ye die, O house of Israel!"

There was a low sound like a murmured prayer, and then Mr. Seixas caught his hat, and without a word left the room.

"May the God of his father Abraham go with him, and abide with him forever!" she said, earnestly; while tears long suppressed ran thick and fast down her cheeks.

The next morning, Isaac came bounding up the avenue, his face glowing with happiness:

"Oh, such good news! *such* good news! my father has begun to pray to Jesus! This morning when we were seated at the table he motioned us to be quiet, and he asked God to bless the food for the sake of the crucified Nazarene. I am so very, very happy, my father is,— he must be a Chrstian, since he prays to Christ. Mother looked astonished, horrified. She could not eat; she only sat and gazed at father as if she thought him out of his right mind. Do come over dear, dear friend, and see my father; you can't imagine how the light shines from his face!"

"I rejoice, with you, my dear boy," she said, gazing in his face with deep affection. "I believe your father has, indeed, become an heir to all the promises God has given to those who seek the Lord their God, and David their king."

She drew him to the closet as she had often done before, and there where they had so many times entreated God to have mercy upon this family, they now poured out their hearts in thanksgiving for the mercies they had received.

"Come with me, please," Isaac urged, when

they had returned to the parlor. Mother is always glad to see you; and I want you to tell her what a blessing has come to our house."

They found Mrs. Seixas weeping bitterly. When Mrs. Duncan took her hand, she burst out afresh: "My husband has renounced his people; he is no longer a Jew."

"Twice a Jew, my dear," he said, tenderly, laying his hand on her head. A Jew by birth and one by faith in the Deliverer of the Jews from the bondage of sin. I never shall renounce my privileges as one of God's chosen people. I glory in them more than ever; but I thank him that I have learned to glory most of all in Him of whom Moses in the law and the prophets did write — in Him who was pierced for my sins, and by whose stripes I am healed."

The little girls presently came dancing into the room, but stopped at sight of their mother's grief.

Isaac caught a hand of each and whispered "go to her and ask *her* to love the Saviour too. Father has begun to love him."

"No! no!! I wish to hear no more!" she shrieked, waving them off in a manner totally unlike her usual loving tones. "You are all against me. What would my father say if he were alive. For his sake at least I will never renounce my religion."

Abigail stood near the door hesitating whether to come in, her countenance looking very sad. Mrs. Seixas noticed her and exclaimed:

"Even Abigail has turned against me. Ben David's words are true, Isaac has become a curse to all in the house. I am cursed because, like Esther, I cannot endure to see the destruction of my kindred."

"You had better leave your mother now," said Mr. Seixas, trying to speak calmly. "She does not mean what she says. We shall bless

God through all eternity for taking Isaac from us for a season, that by his means we might be led into the truth."

The next day the doctor was summoned to his former patient. The excitement had brought on a high fever, which rendered her delirious all night. In the morning she became partially conscious, and exclaimed:

"What is it? What dreadful event has happened?"

Then suddenly recalling the confession of her husband the day before, she burst into an uncontrolled fit of weeping. The physician gave her soothing medicine which produced sleep; but toward night she grew gradually worse until at the close of the second day her situation was alarming.

Her husband watched over her in an agony of grief, his heart lifted up in prayer for the life of her body and the life of her soul.

On the fourth day Mrs. Duncan, who had

been unwearied in her attentions, thought she discovered signs of returning consciousness. She pointed them out to the almost heart-broken husband, and then seeing the poor sufferer slowly unclose her eyes, softly left the chamber. Retiring into an inner apartment, she heard a low sound as of prayer, and presently distinguished the words:

"God of my fathers, of Abraham, Isaac and Jacob, hear my prayer. I have sinned, and done evil all the days of my life; but thou art gracious; thou hast promised pardon and eternal life to all who put their trust in thee. Hear me now for the sake of Him whom the wicked Jews hung on the tree. Grant my petition for this loved one lying so weak and low, that she may live to receive him by faith, into her own heart, who died for her, and to experience the joys granted to thy unworthy servant. This request is made only for the sake of Christ. Amen."

When his prayer was finished, he saw that his wife's eyes were open and fastened upon his. Very tenderly he spoke, thanking the good Father of all, that her consciousness was restored, then rang the bell to summon Abigail to bring some nourishment to the sufferer.

CHAPTER XVII.

A NEW APOSTLE.

MRS. Seixas gained strength very slowly, Every morning her husband knelt by her side, and implored the continuance of God's favor upon them; strength and wisdom for himself in the new path he had begun to tread, and that light from above might dawn on the mind of his beloved companion.

Not once did she allude to events which occasioned her illness, but he could see that she watched them all closely, and was often deeply absorbed in thought.

At last, when she was able to be placed in her lounging chair, which could be made to recline as much as she wished, Mr. Seixas brought his New Testament from the study, and without any comment began to read the account, in John's gospel, the ninth chapter, of Jesus restoring sight to the blind man.

He was greatly encouraged by the interest she manifested, and as he closed the book, said:

"Sophey, if after Isaac was stolen from us we had gone to Jesus with our bleeding hearts, he might have restored him years before. He is indeed worthy to be the Messiah."

She sighed repeatedly, and when she thought herself unnoticed wiped a tear from her eyes.

Myrtilla and Esther had now joined the Infant Sunday School in the village, and the Sabbath, that is the Christian Sabbath, was kept in all its purity.

Mr. Seixas was not a man to be a half-way Christian. After consultation with Mrs. Duncan, who was now regarded as a loved sister, he called upon the clergyman of the parish, and proposed joining himself to the people of God. As soon as Mrs. Seixas's health would allow, he summoned the whole family into her chamber, and set up a family altar where morning and night, prayers and praises were offered, and, we trust, accepted as the sacrifice of humble spirits.

In all his business transactions, too, this new born Israelite sought to bear witness of the grace that was in him. He considered that his wealth was given him for some wise purpose; not to hoard up for his children, but to be used for the advancement of Christ's kingdom.

A man by the name of Nelson had been in his employ for a year. When the family removed to their present home, he was made superintendent of the farming operations. For several weeks, Nelson had been confined to his bed with a fever, prevalent through the town. At the end of the first week, or on Friday night, the time he paid his laborers, when the others came to his library for their wages, Nelson's son came with them.

"What are you here for?" was the stern inquiry. "I owe your father nothing. I have had to hire a man in his place." This was continued week after week; and the boy always returned with the same reply.

But when the love of Christ had entered his soul, he began to inquire whether he had rightly discharged his duties toward his servants. Seizing the first opportnity he visited the sick man at his home, when he was filled with remorse at the destitution he witnessed. The invalid lay in bed, the fever having left him weak and languid, a dark ring around his eyes and his sunken cheeks proving that he had been a great sufferer. His wife sat near him patching an old, threadbare garment, while two boys and one girl were sunning themselves in the doorway.

"Why are you not at school, Ned?" asked Mr. Seixas of the older boy.

Mrs. Nelson answered for him: "I was obliged to sell his clothes to a neighbor to buy medicine for my sick husband."

"Ah! is that the case? How is the poor man to-day?"

"As free from fever as you are, sir; but weak and helpless as a new-born baby. The doctor has left off coming. He said medicine would do no good now. It's good, strengthening food he needs; a cup of good broth and such like."

"And have you given him any?"

She looked the gentleman full in the face.

"No, sir, I haven't a penny to get food with, and there's only a peck and a half of potatoes in the house. At this rate he wont be able to work in a month of Sundays; and how we're to live at all is a wonder. This was said with trembling lips.

"You ought to have let me know how sick he was," returned Mr. Seixas, with a heightened color.

"I thought it enough to send Ned to you on Fridays. I bid the boy say that my husband had worked faithfully for you, and that we were on the point of starving; but he had not the courage to open his mouth."

"I regret exceedingly that he did not; but all that is over now. I have begun to live by a new rule; and I hope I shall be guided to treat my servants better than I have ever done. I want to do my duty to your bodies by giving you wages sufficient to support you comfortably; and I want to watch over your souls, too. There is another life beyond this, you know."

"Praise God," came in a feeble voice from the bed.

"Yes sir, we do know it;" added the woman warmly, "and if it wasn't for the hope of the life beyond, where there will be no sickness nor sorrow, I don't know how we could ever have lived through these weary weeks."

Mr. Seixas was obliged to walk to the door to conceal his emotion; but quickly returned, his pocket book open in his hand.

"Here is the money which ought to have been paid before," he said, putting a roll of bills into the woman's hand; "and Ned must come to the house every day for food to build up his father. I will ask Abigail to find some garments out of which you can make the children clothes for school."

Nelson tried to speak but could only gasp out the words:

"I knew — God would send us aid. I told him this morning how needy we are. You know he says: 'ask and ye shall receive.'"

Mrs. Nelson lifted up both hands while tears rained down her cheeks:

"It's yer faith in the good Lord has done it," she exclaimed eagerly. "Didn't ye tell me this morning the Saviour hadn't forgotten us in our trouble?"

"You must forgive me, Nelson, for my neglect; but indeed, I cannot forgive myself. Come Ned, we'll go now." "He's not fit to walk the streets, sir; but now that I have the means I'll fit him up directly."

Mr. Seixas thought this a good opportunity to teach his children a lesson of charity. So calling Isaac, who had just returned from school, he sent him with his sisters to the cottage, loaded with food and second hand garments. Ned who was near Isaac's size, being completely equipped in a suit the boy had out-grown.

Nor did the work of reformation stop here.

The new-born man made particular inquiries into the situation of each of those in his employ; one man who he found was an infidel, and trying by constant argument to make proselytes to his views, was dismissed, though one of his smartest workmen. Others who had families he encouraged to attend church, offering them the inducement of free seats if they would be regular in their attendance.

"With Isaac he left the privilege of gathering all the children into the Sabbath school, a work which greatly delighted the youth, who soon had enough to form two large classes of pupils.

After Mr. Seixas made a public profession of religion in company with his son and Abigail, the clergyman called upon him with a request that he would take a class in the Sabbath school.

"You forget," said the Hebrew smiling, "that I myself am in need of instruction, being but a babe in knowledge of divine things. True I have the means of learning which some do not possess, being well acquainted with the Hebrew and Greek languages, in which the Bible was written; but there are so many better fitted than I am for the work that I must decline for the present."

Still the pastor pressed him to undertake, urging the benefit of the example.

Mr. Seixas sat silent for a time as if pondering the subject, then said: "I have been trying to do something for the benefit of my workmen who are very numerous, and with their families form quite a little company."

"If some one can be found to take the men, I will form a class of the women, though I imagine I shall have to study diligently to answer some of their questions."

"I will pledge myself," responded the good man, "that if no one else offers, I will teach the men myself."

The next week the two adult classes went into operation, the women, foremost among whom was Mrs. Nelson, occupying the wing slips on the right hand of the pulpit, taught by Mr. Seixas; and their husbands seated on the left of the pulpit under the instruction, not of the pastor, but of his wife.

Weeks passed, and though Mrs. Seixas listened attentively to the daily reading of Scripture; yet she seemed to make no advance toward the end so earnestly desired by her friends.

" It is not with her a matter of conviction," Mr. Seixas remarked to Mrs. Duncan. " It is prejudice, early instilled into all Jews against the name and character of the Nazarene. Blind, wilfully blind, our people have been, rejecting their King, the Lord of Glory. Their Rabbies pronouncing anathemas upon those who dare inquire whether this is 'he of whom Moses in the law and the prophets did write.'"

The lady encouraged him to hope since his wife expressed no opposition to the truth, reminding him that God was ever ready to listen to the prayers of his people, and as sure as his promise was true, would in his own good time grant the earnest request.

Ever since Isaac had been at home he had been in the habit of telling his sisters stories from the Bible for an hour before they retired for the night. The nursery joined his mother's chamber; and as she listened to their childish questions, and heard him so patiently explain over and over again the meaning of the sacred words, she was obliged to confess to herself, there was a power in the Christian religion not found in Judaism.

A good opportunity to compare the two, occurred the first time she rode out. They were driving in the direction of E——, the village where the synagogue was situated, when they saw Rabbi Ben David come out of a Jew's house and walk directly toward them.

The moment of his recognition of them

was very evident, for before that he seemed in high spirits smiling to himself and striking off the heads of grass with his stout cane; but his color changed and his brow darkened as he perceived who was approaching.

Making a motion to the coachman to stop, he advanced directly to the door of the carriage, and began in a loud angry voice to pronounce curses on idolators, worshippers of the Blasphemer, of all Impostors, threatening them with being sent to Gehenna.

When he had spent his rage, he paused and seemed astonished that no opposition was made to this torrent of abuse.

Mr. Seixas was pale, indeed, as pale as he could well be; but his countenance expressed no anger. He only said: "You remember Ben David, King Solomon says: 'the curse causeless shall not come.' I feel no ill will toward my brethren; nor, as you say, have I renounced my birth-right.

"THE CURSE CAUSELESS SHALL NOT COME." Page 226.

I glory in being a Jew. I glory far more in David my king who was foretold by so many of our holy prophets. I believe he has come in the person of our Lord Jesus Christ, and I pray daily that all my brethren may embrace him who was sent for the deliverance of Israel."

Ben David in a rage spat on the ground, but then turning to Mrs. Seixas he said: "I rejoice that you have not departed from the faith of your learned father (blessed be he,)" and then with a haughty wave of the hand he left them.

"Poor, blind, deluded man," murmured the gentleman as they rode on, "hugging to his own heart the curse invoked upon themselves and their children by the wicked Jews who murdered their Lord. What will he do when summoned to appear before the crucified, in whom he will then see the Judge who is to pronounce his doom?"

There was a long silence, during which both seemed absorbed in thought; at last Mrs. Seixas said:

"I was surprised that you did not grow angry, Jesse. You are certainly much changed of late."

"I felt no emotion toward the old man but pity," responded the gentleman in subdued tones. "Lately I felt just as he does. Do you remember how you checked me for speaking so sharply to Isaac the day I came home from prison?"

She sighed repeatedly, and tried to turn her attention to the lovely prospect, but after gazing for some moments in silence at the rich forests gaily dressed in their autumn attire, she said softly as if speaking to herself:

"How hard it is to know what is right!"

"Are you seeking to know that, dear Sophia?" he asked, gazing earnestly in her face. "If so, God will enlighten you and help you to receive the truth.'

"I do not find it so easy to change the whole current of my thoughts as you seem to was the almost petulant reply.

"Ah, you little know the struggles which tore my breast. Many and many a time have I arisen from my couch by your side, without once losing my sorrows in sleep. A growing conviction, arising from my study of the New Testament, that the despised Nazarene, whose name had hitherto been a by-word and reproach, was in reality the Messiah sent of God, only seemed to increase my hatred of him. But thanks be to God, I was not left to my own device. Grace formed the plan of my salvation; and grace compelled me to submit my will to the will of my Redeemer."

CHAPTER XVIII.

FRUITS OF PIETY.

AUTUMN had passed into winter. The two adult classes were merged into one, under the instruction of Mr. Seixas, whose rich store of classical knowledge, together with his acquaintance with Oriental habits and character, rendered his teaching so valuable that many others beside the families of his own workmen, petitioned for admittance; and finally, the class consisting of forty members, adjourned to a small room in the basement of the church, called the pastor's study.

Mr. Seixas had been formerly called by his friends, and he had thought himself a man of leisure. Now he was busy from morning to night.

To him his pastor often pointed as an example of what one man can do in a parish when he is wide awake to the interests of Christ's kingdom. Formerly he was reserved and haughty, both from a natural disinclination to mingle in general society, and still more from a knowledge that the Jews were considered a despised, down-trodden people, and the hatred such a knowledge engendered. Now he was kind and affable to all. There was scarcely a child in the village who did not meet him with a smile, and whose heart did not beat warmer for the kind words sure to be spoken.

After his conversion, feeling himself to be wholly ignorant of the rites and usages of the religion he had professed, he requested his pastor to make a list of the names of books, such as he ought to study, and sent to a bookseller in the city to transmit them to him. He saw too, that his pastor labored " in season and out of season " for the good of his flock, and was shocked when he heard it mentioned in incidental conversation, that he only received the small salary of one thousand dollars a year.

The next morning he sent the good man a check of two hundred dollars which proved indeed a blessing in hour of need.

All this time his petitions for his wife grew more and more fervent; but of late there seemed less reason to hope for her conversion. She was better in health than she had been for years, and being possessed of a thorough education had begun to give her little girls daily lessons, not only in English but in her native Greek. The novelty of her husband's new principles having worn off, she had settled into an apathetic state on the subjects he loved so ardently, though she did one day confess to Mrs. Duncan, that there was something in the Christian's faith which had so changed Jesse that she should scarcely know him. Formerly, though invariably kind and indulgent to her, especially since the loss of Isaac had so shattered her nervous system; yet he was passionate and impulsive in the extreme, often wounding the sensitive hearts of the twins by his sharp reproofs.

. With the servants too, formerly he was often captious, venting his ill humor upon them when his temper was disturbed by outside annoyances. Now he was invariably gentle, administering reproof where it was needed, in love, and with far happier results.

Mrs. Duncan told her the same was true in regard to Isaac, who, ever since she had known him had possessed a passionate temper. Indeed, at first it seemed wholly ungovernable and only yielded to the firmest discipline.

"I remember one instance," she went on,

"when he wanted a banana from a dish of them at dessert, and when I refused him in consequence of the doctor's orders, forbidding fruit for a few days, he threw himself upon the floor and beat his head till I thought he would kill himself."

"How long was this after you had taken him?" was the eager inquiry.

"Not more than three weeks."

"Because it is very strange, for 'Isaac from a babe disliked the taste and even the smell of bananas, complaining that they made his head sick. They always made his father sick too, though he would eat freely of them."

The lady smiled as she answered, "Ever since I have known him he has craved them; and I remember that when the gentleman, whom I supposed was his father, tried to persuade him to remain with me, he would not until a banana was produced from his pocket as a reward for his doing so. While

Isaac ate it, the father, — I mean the uncle, slipped from the room. Isaac only saw him once after, when I took him to the chamber just at dusk."

"More and more wonderful!" murmured the lady. "Did he mourn for his father?"

"At first he did, but much more for his mother, whom he used to call a pet name. I never could exactly make out what it was, but it sounded in his childish tones like, 'Effie,' 'pretty Effie!'"

"No doubt it was Sophy, my husband often called me that."

"Did you pacify him easily?"

"Yes, for the time; but invariably for weeks, he would cry upon going to bed. He seemed to have a dread of it and would scream, 'I don't want to go to sleep, it will kill me like it did my mamma.' I inferred from this, that he had seen his mother lying on the bed after her decease."

"His cruel uncle must have frightened him," exclaimed Mrs. Seixas with more spirit than was often seen in her mild eyes.

In the winter the twins were accidently exposed to the measles, a malignant type of the disease being then prevalent. Esther was taken first, and by early attention was carried safely through the worst stages. On the day when the crisis had passed, Myrtilla fainted at the table. Before night the fever rose very high with no appearance of an eruption. Constant nausea was followed by extreme exhaustion until at the close of the fifth day, the physician announced to the sorrowing parents that he could do no more for the little sufferer.

"Mrs. Duncan however, who spent hours every day by the bed-side of the darling child did not regard the case as hopeless. She had known one similar to this, where a new kind of treatment had to all appearance saved the child's life. Still she had been unwilling to propose so desperate a remedy until all other means had proved useless. Myrtilla lay wholly unconscious, her parched lips apart and her breathing short and oppressive.

Leaving the child in the care of her father, the lady left the room to find Mrs. Seixas and suggest to her that there might still be hope. Softly opening her chamber door she was surprised to find it vacant, but hearing a low sound farther on, she passed through the room supposing her engaged in giving orders to a servant.

But no; it was the voice of prayer, earnest prayer, to the Saviour of sinners, the once despised Nazarene, imploring him who when on earth loved little children, to spare this precious child to her afflicted parents; but if she must leave them, that she might go and dwell in his presence forever.

Mrs. Duncan withdrew from that sacred

spot, her heart bounding with a new joy, and hastened to impart the glad tidings to the anxious husband.

She then proposed to him to wrap Myrtilla in sheets wrung in cold water, after which blankets should be closely folded about her form to induce perspiration.

After some minutes of earnest discussion, Mr. Seixas consented if his wife approved.

In half an hour the little girl had fallen into a sweet, refreshing sleep; and when the doctor came in scarcely expecting to see her alive, he was surprised beyond measure to find her face thickly covered with measles.

From this hour commenced her recovery, and from this hour too, her mother did not hesitate to declare herself a convert to Christianity. Jesus had heard her prayer for her child, she rested on his promise that he would hear her prayer for her own soul.

As soon as Myrtilla was well enough to

sit up, the lady begged her husband to ask the clergyman to come and express for her the gratitude which filled her soul to overflowing.

In due time she too made an open profession of her faith in the Saviour of sinners, greatly to the chagrin of Ben David, who hoped the curses he had pronounced upon her husband, would prevent so feeble a woman from daring to expose herself to the wrath of the Rabbies.

Thus in the enjoyment of home, this now united Christian family passed another year; Isaac spending his time alternately at his two homes, until the period arrived when he must either be sent to a classical school to be fitted for college; or, as his mother preferred, have a tutor at home.

" Mrs. Duncan, however, whose advice was always asked whenever the interests of her boy, as she still called him, were concerned, agreed with his father that if they could find a school of high standard of learning and of well known character for morals, it would be better for him to join it."

The young Hebrew was now a tall handsome youth in his fourteenth year, farther advanced in his classes than most boys of his age, and with a thorough foundation for an English education. Mrs. Seixas having yielded her judgment to that of her husband, it now only remained to be decided where to send him, and for this purpose Mrs. Duncan proposed they should all take a journey through New England, she having an exalted idea of New England Schools, and New England discipline for boys.

Early in June, therefore, they started from home, reaching B—— by easy stages at the close of the fourth day.

From this place they visited several institutions and at last decided in favor of the

P—— Academy in a town about twenty miles from the city. There were many inducements to send a child here, not only on account of the healthiness of the location, the buildings being on a height of land overlooking the country about for nearly fifty miles, but on account of the religious influence emanating from the Theological Seminary on the same ground.

At the public house our whole party spent several days, enjoying greatly the walks and drives in the vicinity of the institution, and then having engaged board for Isaac in a family recommended to them by the Principal, started for home by the way of the Empire city.

Reaching this place on Saturday evening, they went at once to the Astor house, where an event occurred which explained some circumstances heretofore mysterious. But I must not anticipate; I will only say, that during the last year Mr. Seixas had received an answer to a letter he sent at once to the village in France, whence the letter from their old servant had come; this letter had been seen by no one but himself and Mrs. Duncan, to whom he had shown it, to beg her to recall, if possible, the exact time she had received Isaac from his brother, thinking it barely possible that his boy had been carried abroad, and had afterwards been adopted by her.

But she persisted in her first statement and proved conclusively to him that the boy was delivered to her keeping only a few weeks subsequent to his exploit, when he saved her husband from drowning; and this was the exact date of the disappearance of Isaac and his nurse.

CHAPTER XIX.

THE RIGHT SON AT LAST.

THERE were many objects of interest in the great city, and the party intended to remain about a week. One morning on the third day of their stay, Mrs. Duncan, Abigail and Esther, were passing down the wide staircase on their way to the mall, when they met a boy coming up laughing at some remark of the companion he had left. A straw hat of foreign manufacture shaded his eyes, but as he came nearer they all saw that it was Isaac.

Esther gaily caught his hat as he passed, saying: "I've found you out brother. Now come with us for a walk."

The boy started, but Abigail, laughing

heartily, patted him on the shoulder, saying:

"You needn't try to make us believe you don't know us."

"I don't understand you," exclaimed the lad, addressing himself to Mrs. Duncan.

"Come, Isaac," answered the lady, smiling at his feigned surprise. "You have carried the joke far enough, will you join us in a walk?".

"My name is Isaac," said the boy, but you have mistaken me for some other person. I have just arrived in New York from France, and am now going with my mother into the country."

"Who is your mother?" asked the lady, feeling very faint.

"Mrs. Shields, my father is member of Parliament from London."

"Will you come to the parlor for a minute?" asked the lady, feeling unable to stand. "She then sent Abigail to summon her master; thoughts of the letters from France, hitherto considered a forgery, rushing wildly through her mind.

When Abigail entered her mistress' chamber, to her unbounded surprise, she saw Isaac chatting gaily with his parents, and without stopping a moment to reflect, began eagerly to relate what had passed in the hall. Mr. Seixas caught his hat and rushed to the parlor followed almost instantly by his wife and son.

The stranger lad was repeating what he had told her, offering to summon his mother if she wished, when the other Isaac entered.

It was a picture for an artist. The two boys as closely resembling each other as twins rushed forward and stopped when within a few paces and stared.

"I don't wonder you mistook me for this fellow," murmured the stranger, in a slightly foreign accent, "for I can scarcely tell myself which is which. Will you come with me to mother? it's too good a joke for her to lose."

But Mr. Seixas would not permit either of the boys out of his sight. There was a certain look about the stranger, occasioned by a dimple in his chin which caused a rush of memories, filling him with the conviction that this Isaac, and not the other, was his own child.

"Mother, mother, don't look so," exclaimed our Isaac, seizing Mrs. Seixas's hand; but she did not hear him, her eyes were fastened on the other lad with a look of mingled surprise and horror.

"Where did you come from?" she asked eagerly; then without waiting for a reply she burst out with a passionate flood of tears: "Jesse, this is our boy; our precious, lost Isaac."

She fell back almost fainting, when the lad

threw himself on his knees beside her, and with his face upturned to Mr. Seixas, asked in a tone of intense anxiety:

"Am I a Jew, then?"

"I have no doubt of it. But where is the lady you call mother? I must see her at once."

He gave the gentleman the number of the room, who instantly sent a servant to ask her presence in the parlor.

"My father, Mr. Shields, will be in presently," added the lad; "but all this is very strange!"

Mrs. Shields was a French lady, and conversed with quite an accent. As she had not the slightest conception of the scene transacting below, her surprise may be conceived on seeing her son kneeling by the side of a fainting lady; and another youth, the exact image of the first, standing by, looking from one to another as if wondering what would happen next.

In her excitement she began to talk in French, and rattled off question after question to her son, who answered eagerly in the same language.

It was some time before Mr. Seixas could learn from her that this was a child she had seen in a convent near Nice; that she had adopted him and treated him like an own son; that his father had made a will giving him a handsome fortune; that she had received him from a gentleman who told her his parents were dead, and that she wouldn't give him up.

"Can you tell me where his nurse is now?" queried the gentleman, trying to control his agitation.

"Yes, she came to us a short time before we left home. She told me Isaac had a mother living, and a father too, and she gave me

.the clothes he had on when he was in the convent."

"Oh, where are they!" exclaimed Mrs. Seixas, starting from the sofa.

"At home of course! They are too small for him now, and I did not bring them with me."

"Can you tell me what they are?"

"Yes; a black hat with a red plume tipped with black; a velvet tunic, — and Isaac, oh Isaac! you have the stud which fastened the little shirt in front, in your bosom now."

"Yes, mother. It is marked I. S."

Mr. Seixas clasped the boy in his arms, murmuring: "God be praised, my son! my long lost son! we have met again.

"And God be praised, I have my own boy back again," ejaculated Mrs. Duncan, seizing her Isaac's hand.

Mrs. Seixas laughed and cried, and smelt her salts, and felt as she afterwards expressed it, as if all the world were turning to Isaacs.

"But I shall never give him up," urged the French lady putting down her foot in a decided manner." My husband will be here soon, and he will tell you, one Isaac is enough for you. This boy is ours."

It was all in vain that the gentleman explained that this child was stolen from them years before. She either could not, or would not, understand; but continually pointed to the other Isaac, saying: "You have one, you must be satisfied."

Mr. Shields came in later, and confirmed the lady's account. He had received the child from Mr. Justin Seixas; and they had always supposed him to be an orphan until the visit of his old nurse, who had become a mother, and who now could sympathize with the parents in their grief at their child's loss.

Mr. Seixas related the remarkable circumstances attending their discovery of the other

Isaac; the possibility that his brother had been married and had a son near the same age never having occurred to him; and the singularity of the dimple in the chin so closely resembling his mother's, while Mrs. Seixas clung convulsively to the lad exclaiming: "He is mine, my own! I feel it here," putting her hand to her heart.

The next day when all were more calm, Mrs. Duncan referring to what Mr. Justin Seixas had told her, remarked: "I have been thinking it all over, and I have come to the conclusion that he told me the truth. Isaac was his son, near the same age with your boy. For some reasons of his own, he had concealed his marriage, and now that his wife was dead, it was easier for him to flee the country; but he did not wish the care of two children, and revenge prevented him from leaving your child where you might discover him. It is easy now to explain why the boy I loved so well, had such an undisciplined temper."

"Yes, and I am glad that in his dying moments my brother did not deceive me. He told me the boy was in a village in France; but his strength failed before he could name the place."

"Well, you will have your boy; and I mine; but I pity the poor French lady."

Mr. Seixas smiled; "I think she will soon recover her cheerfulness," he said. "Did you see how gaily she flirted with that whiskered foreigner at breakfast? But I am most anxious to know the character of my boy. He seems pleased at the late discovery, though evidently chagrined at finding himself a Jew."

"How wonderful are the ways of Jehovah!" remarked the lady devoutly. "We must all labor and pray for the conversion of this dear youth."

Hon. Mr. Shields soon convinced his wife

that her claim to Isaac was invalid; and therefore she yielded him up, and consoled herself with the society of the numerous foreigners at the hotel.

As to the boy himself, Mrs. Duncan could not discover signs of much feeling, either of regret at parting from those who had taken the place of parents, or of joy at being restored to his own kindred. He seemed indeed, pleased with his little sisters whose beauty attracted much attention; but in a day or two wearied of their caresses, saying as they hung around him:

"Get away! Girls are such a bother!"

"I love our old Isaac the best," faltered Myrtilla, after such a rebuff. "He never shakes off my arm, nor speaks cross."

"Be patient, my dear," answered Mrs. Duncan. "Remember he is almost a stranger yet."

"I don't believe he is a bit good either,"

added the greived child. " He says real bad words. I heard him asking that other mother for money, and when she only gave him a little, and told him not to trouble her any more, because he had another father and mother he said awful bad words."

CHAPTER XX.

VISIT TO THE RABBI.

WHEN the news of the restoration of the true son of Mr. Seixas reached Rabbi Ben David, a smile of exultation passed over his features. It was quite a triumph to him that the boy Isaac whom he had cursed, would not be raised to wealth and rank; but a few moments reflection lessened this feeling, or rather changed it to one of keen regret.

" If the follower of the blashphemer (cursed be he) had kept out of the way a little longer," was his angry ejaculation, " Jesse Seixas would have remained true to the religion of his fathers, Abraham, Isaac and Jacob. Now he has become a vile apostate, and alas, wholly alienated from those who lead God's chosen people!"

The fervent sigh which accompanied the last words, proved the sincerity of Ben David's regret at the loss of the loaves and fishes, which, as the chief Rabbi of the Jews in that neighborhood, he had been accustomed to receive from the wealthy Israelites.

Among this class no one had given with a more liberal hand than Mr. Seixas, scarcely a week having passed without some token of remembrance being conveyed from his house to that of the Rabbi. Indeed if the whole truth were told, it was by such acts as these, the gentleman sought to stifle the voice of conscience which often told him that no atoning sacrifice had been offered for his sins.

On the occasion when we last met the Rabbi, the carriage containing the family of Mr. Seixas was scarcely out of sight before he repented having been so carried away by passion as to lose the favor of this wealthy friend; and months as they rolled on only made the repentance more bitter. In his worldly estate Ben David was far from rich. His wife was a confirmed invalid; and his four sons inclined to be wayward and extravagant.

For a long time he had been trying to form some plan wherein he might re-instate himself in the favor of the apostate without compromising his own faith; and after an hour's reflection on the strange intelligence that this Isaac, he had seen, was only nephew instead of son to his former friend, he concluded that now was the time for him to act.

It was with no little astonishment, therefore, that one morning soon after they reached home, Isaac Duncan as we sha'l once more call him, brought from the office a curiously folded epistle which upon opening was found to contain two notes of invitation. These were severally addressed to "Isaac son of Jesse," and "Isaac son of Justin Seixas."

"What can it mean?" exclaimed the boy, advancing eagerly to his mother's side, his face flushing crimson.

Mrs. Duncan calmly read aloud, as follows:

"To Isaac child of Abraham:

A meeting of Jewish youth will convene in the vicinity of my house on the fourteenth of the seventh month, where thy company will be very acceptable. Thy worthy uncle will tell thee that we meet to celebrate the feast of ingathering, according to the command of the Lord given our fathers.

Ben David."

Mrs. Duncan could not help laughing when she saw the look of horror on her boy's face.

"You are not obliged to accept the invitation, my dear," she said gaily. "Still I think it might be pleasant. I devoutly wish he had included me in his invitation."

"Oh, mother! you can't tell how very"—

"Stop, my child," interrupted the lady playfully, putting her hand on his mouth. "You must remember, that, it was a terrible sin in his estimation, for you to apostatize from the faith of your fathers."

"I wonder what my cousin will say," rejoined the boy, "I'll see him at once, and give him his note."

He took up the envelope again, and now saw in the corner some beautifully written Hebrew words.

"I'll ask uncle Jesse, what these mean," he said in an excited tone. "Oh, I wish I could read Hebrew!"

Mr. Seixas and Isaac were in his study

when the boy entered. The gentleman read the note with a very arch smile.

"I expected he would relent," he said at last. "Well, what does your mother say?"

"She thinks I should enjoy it. She wants to go herself, sir; but I've seen enough of the old Rabbi."

"I'll go at any rate," exclaimed Isaac Seixas in a loud, decided tone. "I should like to see the old fellow. Is he jolly?"

"I suppose your cousin would scarcely call him so," replied his father smiling. "He is a very learned man, every whit a Jew; and until we apostatized, as he calls it, proved every way an agreeable friend."

"Shall we write an acceptance, father? for I'm bent on making Ben David's acquaintance," eagerly exclaimed Isaac.

It took a good deal of urging however, before Isaac Duncan yielded his wish to his cousin's; and Mr. Seixas would only consent if they went together. Then the gentleman wrote a friendly answer saying that he would himself, accompany the boys to the Rabbi's house some day during the week.

It was at last decided that the cousins should go on Wednesday, and remain until Saturday night, that Isaac Seixas might have an opportunity which he greatly desired, of attending the service of the synagogue.

The morning was a lovely one, just the day for a festival. Isaac Seixas was in high spirits, anticipating great fun in watching the peculiarities of Ben David, upon which both Myrtilla and Esther had been quite eloquent. Indeed, Myrtilla regarded their visit somewhat in the light of a leap into a den of a lion.

Isaac Duncan found himself wondering what could be the motive of the Rabbi, in inviting them, and lifted his heart in prayer to his Heavenly Friend for wisdom to guide his conversation aright.

It was about nine o'clock when they started on their expedition. They were scarcely seated in the carriage when Isaac Duncan said: "uncle Jesse will you please explain about the Feast of Tabernacles?"

"Yes, you remember the Hebrew words in your letter. They were "Feast of Tabernacles, Deuteronomy 16; 13, 14, 15." This feast which is also called the feast of ingathering, because it is after the gathering in of the corn and the wine, began last Sabbath and lasts till the close of the next Sabbath being eight days."

"But uncle Jesse," exclaimed Isaac, opening his pocket Bible at the chapter mentioned. It says here that the feast was to be observed in the seventh month, September is the ninth month."

But, my boy, the Jewish year is reckoned from the month of Nisan which is March. New Year's day is the first day of Nisan.

Counting from that, Tisri or September is the seventh month.

"Formerly this feast was anticipated with great delight by all the Jews; but for many years, our people have grown slack in their religious observances. Ben David is however very strict in adhering to the rites and ceremonies of his fathers.

"This is the year of release, or Jubilee, when every slave, taken from among the Hebrews, is made free. It occurs every seventh year and is fully regarded. This afternoon you will go with the Rabbi to the encampment where the booths or tents are pitched, and listen as he reads aloud in the hearing of all the Israelites there assembled, the whole ceremonial law."

"Mother has often told me about the booths. She says they were made of beautiful trees."

"Yes, and of thick leaved branches; where

palms grow they are greatly preferred; willows of the brooks are also used. It is a season of great festivity and rejoicing. The poor are provided with the same food as the most wealthy and all are commanded to rejoice together, because, as the Scripture says, "the Lord thy God shall bless thee in all thine increase, and in all the works of thine hands, therefore, thou shalt surely rejoice."

"Wasn't this the feast, sir, where offerings were made?"

"Yes, every one who is able, will carry a free-will offering, to be used for the poor and necessitous among them."

"I can imagine, then, what is in the large hamper under the driver's feet," exclaimed Isaac Seixas, laughing merrily. "It is a free will offering."

"You will see," urged his father with a smile, and at this minute they reached Ben David's house.

There was a loud cackling of geese in the barn yard at the end of the garden, which caused Mr. Seixas to say:

"You know, Isaac, that the fat of geese is used extensively among the Jews instead of lard, which is forbidden. There are many other customs peculiar to our nation that you will see here. Nothing will please Ben David better than to explain them to you.

The Rabbi as they expected was gone to the encampment, but had left word that he would return for his young friends.

Mr. Seixas only stopped to take from the hamper a huge package, upon which Isaac caught sight of the name Ben David, and then drove away in the direction of the booths. The house was a large one with a front door common to the two families residing in it. It was at once evident to the lads that something unusal had occurred; and presently the wife of the Rabbi, a very feeble looking woman, told them that a child had just died in the house of her neighbor.

She had scarcely finished relating the sad circumstance, when a man came in and seeing the boys asked:

"Are you Jews?"

"Yes," answered Isaac Duncan, unhesitatingly.

"Can you come and help us?"

"Yes."

The lady remonstrated, but the man was in haste, and answered:

"It is impossible to get other help, every man is at the feast."

Curious to know in what their help was desired, the boys readily followed to the room which contained the body of the child. The infant lay where it did when it breathed its last; but it now was to be washed and prepared for burial.

Isaac's thoughts recurred to what his

mother had told him as he watched the man's movements, especially the great care taken to avoid touching the dead body, and whispered to his cousin, that to touch a corpse rendered any Jew unclean according to the ceremonial aw.

Obeying the orders of their companion, the boys assisted to remove the corpse to the centre of the room, where they placed it on a board, under which large tubs were set. This being done the man poured several pails of water over the body without uncovering it. He then proceeded to wash by rubbing the sheet up and down over the surface. When he thought this accomplished, he directed the boys to take hold of each end of a sheet and hold it over the corpse while he drew away the wet one, charging them repeatedly, not to look on the face of the dead. The body was then rubbed dry through the sheet; another fresh one was substituted; and then the young assistants were dismissed.

CHAPTER XXI.

FEAST OF TABERNACLES.

THEY had scarcely returned to the parlor where Ben David's wife awaited them when the Rabbi came hastily in, greatly flurried and out of breath with his walk, and greeted his guests with much cordiality. He had seen and spoken with Mr. Seixas; and it was evident was delighted with the result of his scheme. When he had received and examined the package, his pleasure was exhibited in a manner almost childish. He repeatedly patted both the boys on their shoulders, exclaiming:

"Just the thing! Capital! Good! Good!"

Before he grew calm enough to talk of accompanying his guests to the fields, they were quite as much disgusted with his familiarity, as Isaac Duncan had formely been with his fierceness.

The sight presented as they approached the encampment, was as beautiful as it was novel. The booths or tents were variously made according to the taste and skill of the occupant, while every where branches of trees were suspended like flags from soldiers' tents.

Ben David escorted his young companions to a booth at the farther extremity of the ground, where he introduced them to his sons, two of whom Isaac Duncan recognized as the lads he had seen playing marbles in the synagogue.

After joining in quite a sumptuous repast, the boys followed the Rabbi to another booth open in front, where he stood for two long hours and read in a hurried irreverent manner from the sacred scrolls containing the ceremonial law.

Very little attention was paid to this, certainly not by the younger part of the audience. In all rude attempts to divert attention from the reading, Abner and Samuel the elder sons of the Rabbi were foremost; and Isaac Duncan as he witnessed their sly jokes, their tricks of pinching, tickling their companions, or snapping apple seeds into their ears, could not help thinking of old Eli and his wicked sons Hophi and Phineas.

Before the Jewish Sabbath, our young friends become heartily sick of living in a booth; indeed Isaac Seixas was with difficulty persuaded by his cousin to remain until Saturday night when his father's carriage would be sent for them.

On Friday evening just as the village clock struck five, the boys observed a great commotion among the people. Many of them began to gather up into bundles sundry articles they had used during the week while others made some slight preparation of the food already cooked for the last day of the feast, the approaching Sabbath.

Isaac's curiosity was now fully roused He related to his cousin an incident which had occured at one time when he and his uncle made a call on a Jewish friend. They entered the house an hour or two after the commencement of the Sabbath, or about eight o'clock Friday night. To their astonishment they found the family sitting in the dark. The lady apologized, but made no attempt to light the lamps, until the return of a Gentile servant who had been on an errand. When Isaac inquired of his father the reason for this delay, he was told that lighting the lamps was considered work and could not therefore be performed without breaking the command to do no work.

The answer was entirely satisfactory until at a later hour the lady said to Mr. Seixas:

"I am glad you came in. I was quite low-spirited and was just urging my husband to go to the theatre."

Such an inconcistency as this led the two Isaacs to be on the *qui vive* for any new developments. There was a trumpet sounded at the moment the sun disappeared beneath the horizon; but except this the boys saw no indications of holy rest. Indeed the sons of the Rabbi seemed more than ever ready for their low pranks.

At last Ben David came to their tent and sat down. Perhaps he remembered that since the first hour his visitors arrived he had paid them very little attention; certainly he now appeared unusually gracious.

"Is this exactly the way the Feast of Tabernacles was celebrated in old times?" inquired Isaac Duncan.

The old man sighed, but presently answered; "Similar, very similar."

"Will you tell my cousin, sir, about the sounding of the rams horns for the commencement of the Jewish Sabbath?"

The Rabbi roused at this, and holding himself very erect, began:

"Those were in the days of Israel's glory, when on every altar were bulls and goats; when the High Priest walked in state, with his breast-plate glittering in the sun; when all difficulties were settled by an appeal to the urim and thummim."

Unconciously to himself Ben David's voice took a lofty tone, but soon recovering himself he added:

"But you asked me to describe the keeping of the Sabbath.

After the evening sacrifice, or about three o'clock on the sixth day of the week a man mounted to the watch tower, and sounded two long, loud, clear notes. This was a signal to the people that it was time for the work of preparation to commence.

"Their preparation consisted partly in cleaning their houses and washing their persons; and partly in preparing the viands on which they were to regale themselves on the holy day. No persons except tailors, shoemakers and scribes, were permitted to extend their ordinary work into the hours of preparation, or after the sounding of the rams horns: and this was because one class prepared the bodies; and the other instructed the minds of their brethren, for the Sabbath rest.

"All others, master, mistress and servant, worked heartily, cleaving wood, sweeping floors, chopping herbs, and preparing the food."

"These rules were held so sacred that a law was passed by the Roman Emperor exempting the Jews from obeying a summons into court during the hours of preparation or until the close of their Sabbath."

"About six o'clock when the sun was setting, the horns sounded again. This was the signal for lighting the Sabbatical lamps in all the houses, a duty which devolved on the women, who also were required to keep them burning until the close of the Sabbath. If any were so poor that they had no oil, they asked it of the rich."

"In the morning every one dressed in the best clothes he had, which were called Sabbatical garments, after which they ate breakfast."

With the rich all the meals were sumptuous; and even the poor who lived on alms, during the Sabbath shared the bounty of their richer neighbors.

"The first duty after breakfast was to attend a public prayer in the Synagogue, after which they returned to dinner. When this meal was concluded, they frequently occupied the time until supper by going to hear a discourse on divinity from some one of their learned scribes. After this they ate and drank until three stars of considerble magnitude became visible in the firmament. This was the sign of the departure of the Sabbath. Spices were then prepared in each family for the refreshment of those who might faint with sorrow at the termination of so joyful a day, and over these spices the master of the house pronounced the *habdalah* or blessing of separation, and the ceremonies of the day were concluded."

Both the boys thanked Ben David for giving them so interesting an account; and they ever afterward considered this the most pleasant part of their celebration of the Feast of Tabernacles.

Mr. and Mrs. Seixas had been in their own home only a few months before they were greived to find that their son had no principles of honesty or truthfulness.

"If either were Justin's son," exclaimed the gentleman, "this boy seems to inherit his traits to the life."

"I think it is the training," was Mrs. Duncan's earnest response. "My boy was ungovernable in temper, while he had not the slightest idea of the sin of lying. It was a gradual work requiring great patience and wisdom to teach him to control himself by the law of God. But for divine grace, I never could have accomplished it."

"Now you have your reward," was the feeling response. "I think his influence over his cousin will be great."

"God grant it may be. It will be a great trial for me to part with him, now that I know he is mine, my own."

"Mrs. Duncan, we shall have reason through all eternity to bless God that you lent him to us for two years. All that I may be enabled to accomplish for God and my fellow men, I owe to —"

"Divine grace," she said interrupting him: and to that grace you must recommend your son. Pray for him, and with him. Let him see that religion is an every day garment not assumed by you, as is too often the case with Christians for Sunday wear."

"I hope you will not be wearied if Sophia and I often come to you for advice."

"Never: let the lad go in and out as my boy does. I have already tried to win his confidence, and it will be a happiness to me to give you all the aid in my power. Still nothing can take the place of parental authority. Your son has had unlimited indulgence. It will not be easy to restrain him, but it must be done, or he will be ruined. Talk kindly but firmly with him; let him see that what you desire is his best good, from a habit of implicit obedience, and by the blessing of the God of his fathers, you will have your reward.

The Elmwood Series.

4 vols. 16mo. Illustrated. In neat box.

PRICE, - - - - - - - - $5.00.

THE MILL-AGENT.

By Mrs. MARY A. DENNISON.

"The more of this class of books the better. It is one of the best-told and most interesting Temperance tales that has yet appeared. The style is very graphic and life-like, and the story is powerfully written and very affecting."

1 vol. 16mo. Illustrated. Price, $1.25.

OUT OF PRISON.

By Author of "Mill-Agent."

Another work of rare originality and merit. It is an admirable book; not only for the noble conceptions of the right and true which hallow its pages, but for the beauty of its personations of character, and the genial spirit which pervades the whole.

1 vol. 16mo. Price, $1.50.

The Huntingdons; or, Glimpses of Inner Life.

By Mrs. MARIA LOUISA HAYWARD. 1 vol. 16mo. Price, $1.75.

"We cheerfully commend this volume as one which will not only interest youthful readers, but will leave an impression on their minds which will make them better for having read it."

HORACE WELFORD.

A collection of short moral stories for the young. The book is profusely illustrated, and cannot fail of being attractive to youth.

1 vol. 16mo. Price, $1.00.

HENRY A. YOUNG & CO.,

(SUCCESSORS TO GRAVES & YOUNG,)

24 CORNHILL, BOSTON, MASS.

www.ingramcontent.com/pod-product-compliance
Lightning Source LLC
Chambersburg PA
CBHW032110230426
43672CB00009B/1693